The Last of the Puffermen
THE REAL WORLD OF PARA HANDY

I would like to dedicate this book to all the men still
alive today who worked and sailed on the puffers prior to 1970,
as you truly are 'The Last of the Puffermen'.

Edward Keith McGinn

The Last of the Puffermen

THE REAL WORLD OF PARA HANDY

KEITH McGINN

Neil Wilson Publishing Ltd.
www.nwp.co.uk

NWP

Neil Wilson Publishing Ltd
Suite Ex 8, The Pentagon Centre
44 Washington Street
GLASGOW
G3 8AZ

Tel: 0141-221-1117
Fax: 0141-221-5363
E-mail: info@nwp.co.uk
http://www.nwp.co.uk

A catalogue record for this book is available
from the British Library.

ISBN 978-1-897784-99-0

First published in October 2007

Typeset in Joanna
Designed by Mark Blackadder

Printed and bound WS Bookwell, Finland.

Contents

Acknowledgements

I would like to thank, most sincerely, all the people who helped and encouraged me in the writing of this book. Len Paterson edited my manuscript, added photographs and made the book much more complete than I could ever have envisaged. He also kindly contributed the introduction. My thanks are also due to Neil Wilson for taking on my work and turning it into a published book. To Captain Andy Milner and his colleague Ann MacDonald who typed my original hand-written effort and sorted out my spelling mistakes, to my brother-in-law, Professor Jim Rhodes and to Andy Low who read my early writings and encouraged me to carry on writing, my grateful thanks.

Last, but not least, thanks to my wife, Jo, who put up with me sailing on the puffers for all those years and tolerated me being away from home most of our married life.

E.K. McG.

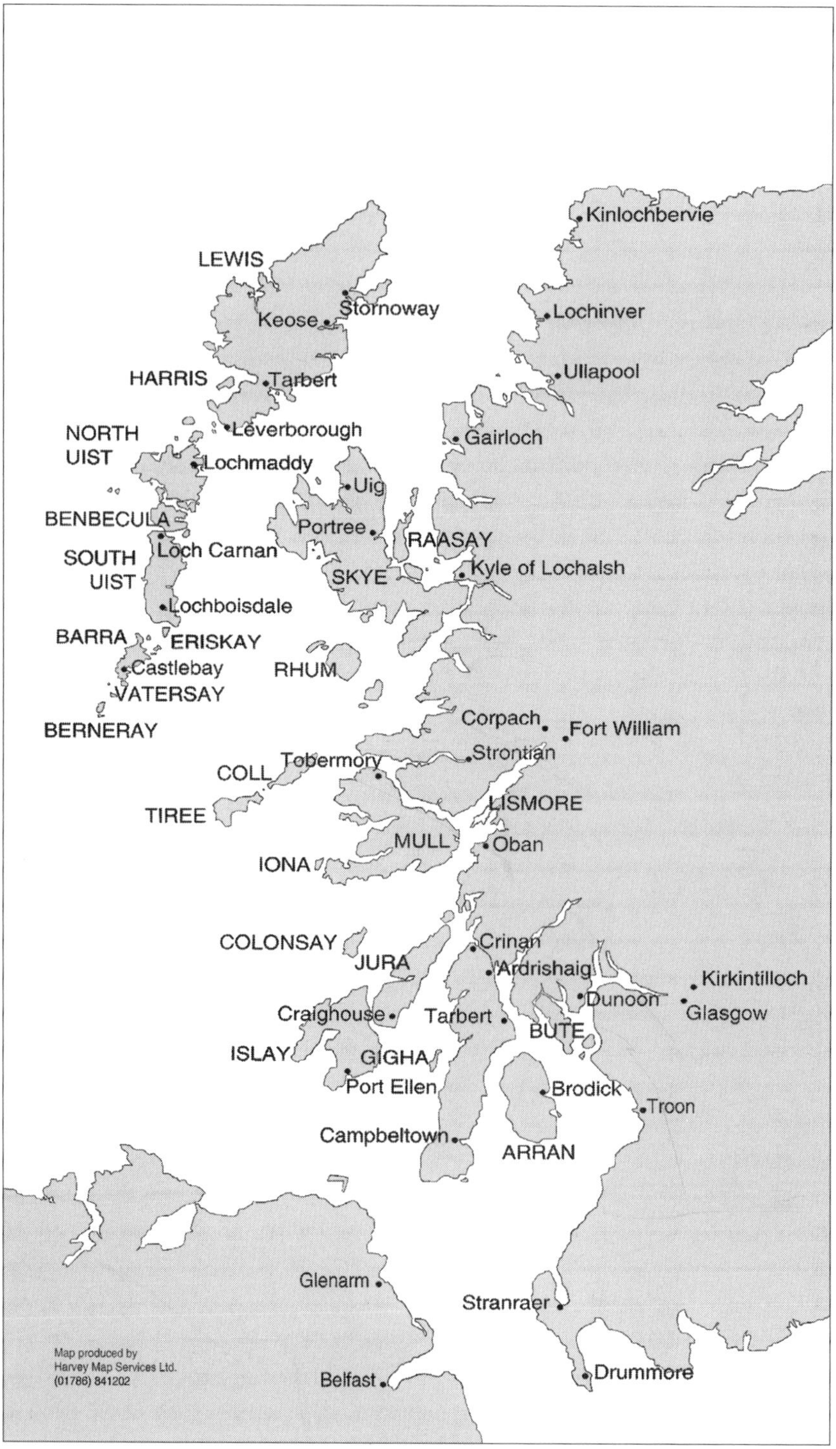

Kinlochbervie

LEWIS

Keose • Stornoway

Lochinver

HARRIS • Tarbert

Ullapool

NORTH UIST • Leverborough

Gairloch

• Lochmaddy

BENBECULA

• Uig

SOUTH UIST Loch Carnan

Portree • RAASAY

SKYE • Kyle of Lochalsh

• Lochboisdale

BARRA ERISKAY

• Castlebay RHUM

VATERSAY

BERNERAY

Corpach • Fort William

COLL Tobermory Strontian

TIREE LISMORE

MULL • Oban

IONA

COLONSAY Crinan

JURA • Ardrishaig Kirkintilloch

• Dunoon

Craighouse • Tarbert Glasgow

ISLAY GIGHA BUTE

• Port Ellen Brodick Troon

Campbeltown • ARRAN

Glenarm •

Stranraer •

Map produced by
Harvey Map Services Ltd.
(01786) 841202

Belfast • Drummore

Introduction

Keith McGinn speaks with the authentic voice of the pufferman. He worked on these small boats that serviced the West Highlands and Islands of Scotland from the 1960s to the closure of the trade in 1994.

He worked as a deckhand on the last days of the 66-ft canal boats, (the classic puffer design) and eventually became a skipper in charge of a coaster, still working on the West Coast, that could carry five times the cargo of the small vessel in which he started his career. He tells his 'warts-and-all' story as it was. He does not glamorise the life though he enjoyed good times and companionship. He does not minimise the dangers, tragedies and hardships either. He lived and worked in unique times and in a real sense he is one of the last of the puffermen.

For about 20 years of the time he describes I was part of the management team at Glenlight Shipping Ltd, one of the last of the puffer companies. My part in this book has been to structure the narrative, add some footnotes and this introduction by way of explanation for the general reader.

Glenlight Shipping Ltd was formed in 1968 by uniting the interests of the two larger long-established puffer companies, Hay-Hamilton Ltd. and Ross & Marshall Ltd., who came together after they lost their trade to Islay with the advent of the roll-on-roll-off ferries. The presence of the publicly subsidised ferries and the increasing trend to use road transport depressed freight rates for the puffers to the point where the business of servicing the West Highlands became unprofitable. This happened despite Glenlight investing heavily in larger ships to try to reap the benefits of the economies of size as Keith describes.

Yet the ferries could not effectively carry the bulk commodities that the Highlands and Islands needed. In 1980 an accommodation was reached with the Scottish Office under the Highlands Shipping Act to directly subsidise the trade and also reduce the cost to the cargo recipient through the Tariff Rebate Subsidy. This was achieved at a fraction of the cost of subsidising the ferries. Government terminated this arrangement in 1994 precipitating the closure of the puffer trade. Keith and his fellow seamen became redundant.

Keith records in the final chapter, 'The bosses fought like hell to keep the firm going and save our jobs.' We tried. Thanks for the compliment, Keith.

Len Paterson, September 2007

CHAPTER 1

The Start

My introduction to the puffers came in the summer of 1965. At that time, I worked for Ayr Burgh Water Department at their treatment plant at Knockjarder, outside Dalrymple, near Ayr, in the days before regionalisation.

A new family had moved to the village. Hughie Gibson got a start at the waterworks; so he and I were paired together on any two-man jobs. He was a good laugh and very streetwise. Hughie had a young family of four kids to bring up but I soon found out that he was not very enthusiastic about work. After being there for about a month, he asked me one day, 'What age are you?'

'Twenty-one' I replied.

'No, no', he said, 'you can't be, you are about fifty-two or fifty-three!'

'I'm twenty one past on 4th February, I was born in 1944,' I replied but he said he had heard me talking in the bothy with old Connel, Jimmy Barr, Sandy Wallace and Archie MacGregor (all men in their late fifties).

'Did you see Corrie last night? That was some row between Elsie Tanner and Ena Sharples; poor old Minne Caldwell, she was in the middle of it; and did you watch Wagon Train? That was a good story. What do we get tonight, Tuesday? That's

The Puffer. The *Sealight*, seen here in the Upper Harbour, Glasgow, was built in 1930 at Ferguson's yard, Port Glasgow for Ross & Marshall Ltd. She is a typical example of the pre-World War II steam lighter and of a design that had changed little for a quarter of a century. Her 66-ft length and 18-ft beam meant that she could pass through the locks of the Forth and Clyde and Crinan canals. She could carry about 120 tons of coal when fully loaded.

There was no enclosed wheelhouse and the helmsman was exposed to the elements, though he could be partly protected by a canvas dodger. Both the mast and the funnel could be lowered to allow her to pass under the bridges seen in the background. Her 34-ft long cargo hatch was closed by wooden hatch boards made waterproof by a tarpaulin held in place by wooden chocks.

In the bow was the steam-driven winch which operated her cargo lifting gear. The derrick is seen lying down the centre line of the vessel and resting on the top of the engine-room casing. Underneath this area, in the focsle, was the cramped accommodation for three men, in a space about 15-ft long. The davit, used for raising and lowering both the anchor and the lifeboat, is seen on the left side at the bow.

For economic reasons in the 1950s these vessels were superseded by diesel-driven puffers of some 80-ft length which could be accommodated in the locks of the Crinan. At the same time, and for the same reasons, some of the 66-ft steam puffers were converted to diesel propulsion and the re-design of the aft end, made possible by the removal of the boiler and coal bunkers, allowed for the provision of improved crew accommodation.

The *Lady Isle* and *Lady Morven*, the ships of the Irvine Shipping and Trading Company, in which the author first went to sea in the 1960s, were diesel conversions of steam puffers. *Courtesy of the Ballast Trust*

1

Emergency Ward 10 and tomorrow we get Corrie and then Z Cars. Did you hear wee Isa Smith won £10 at the bingo on Saturday night? Aye! She had to use the money to bail her son out on Sunday morning! Big May's still going out with Tommy Robertson. If Tommy's wife finds out she'll tear Big May's heid off!'

'You're talking like these old men, village gossip and what's on TV! Get a life!! I hope you are not going to stay at this type of work for the next forty odd years, you'll be an old man before your time,' I replied.

I had tried to join the Merchant Navy but had left it too late to get on deck and didn't fancy a fireman's job. Hughie suggested that I write to a few companies and he told me about the coal boats that sailed out of Troon and Ayr. I borrowed a telephone book and wrote down six or seven addresses and sent letters off to them. I didn't hear anything for about five months. Then I received a letter from the Irvine Shipping Company[1] asking if I still wanted to go to sea. If so, would I come to the Irvine office for an interview? This I did in December 1965. As I didn't have any sea experience, Mr. Campbell[2] didn't seem too keen to start me and said he would be in touch. Aye, right!

On the office walls there were a few framed photographs of ships which I quickly glanced at on my way out and thought 'Not bad. I was looking forward to becoming a sailor.' I never heard any word about a job and had telephoned a couple of companies to be told they didn't take men with no experience or without a discharge book, whatever that was!

I cycled home from work one night, about the middle of May 1966, to find there was a letter for me from the Irvine Shipping Company asking if I still wanted a job as a deckhand on one of their ships. (The photographs on the office walls flashed through my mind.) 'Yes! Definitely!' I had to telephone Mr Campbell at his home after six o'clock and he was to give me instructions on when and where to join. I rushed my dinner and jumped on my bike and cycled the two miles back to Dalrymple to telephone. Mr Campbell wanted to know if I could join tomorrow (Tuesday). I wanted to say 'yes', but really needed to hand in a week's notice, or at least four days. I could join any time after that. He thought the ship was only doing a short run and would be back in Troon on Monday but asked me to telephone on Friday night and he would confirm this. I handed in my notice on Tuesday morning, after four and a half years with the water department.

Hughie Gibson had long gone. Coronation Street, Wagon Train, Z Cars and the local gossip were still number one talking points. I would miss it. I telephoned on Friday night and was told to join the *Lady Isle* on Monday morning at 0800 in Troon. This was the 31st May 1966.

On Sunday night I packed my bag with my working gear, boots and clean travel clothes. I didn't really know what to take as this was my first venture into

---

1 *Irvine Shipping and Trading Co. Ltd.*
2 *RS Campbell, Managing Director.*

the outside world. What a shock it was to be! My old man's only words to me were:

'What time are you leaving?'

'Six o'clock.'

'Well, don't make a bloody noise at that time of day.'

Thanks Dad, I love you too. Mum was her usual quiet self and promised not to get up and make me a breakfast but I knew it was really because she didn't like to say goodbyes.

I left the house at six o'clock, walked up past the pond that was in front of the house where a couple of ducks were swimming. The crows and jackdaws were going about their business, the sun was shining through the trees as I climbed over the gate into the field that would take me to the main road and the two-mile walk to Dalrymple. (There were no buses on this road.) I carefully watched where I put my feet crossing the field as I didn't want to smell of cow dung, which has a nasty habit of sticking to your boots and clothes. Being a country boy I probably smelt that way anyway.

On down past Dales Farm I could see them taking the milk cows in. Dunree Farm had already started milking but they had a bigger herd. I had about half-a-mile to walk to the village; my bag was getting heavier and I began to think that my sisters had put bricks into it while I was sleeping. I arrived at the village in plenty of time for the bus. I met Andy Samson who asked me where I was going.

'I've got a job as a deckhand on a ship,' I replied.

'Are you going off to Glasgow to join?' Andy asked.

'No. Just up to Troon,' I said.

'I didn't know there were any ships came into Troon. I sometimes work up in Troon Harbour and the only things I've seen are these dirty wee coal boats that go round the islands. Yer off yer heid joining them!' Andy retorted.

At that the bus arrived for Ayr.

CHAPTER 2

Lady Isle

I reached Troon Harbour, which was a hive of activity. Coal wagons were being shunted and lorries and cars were moving. I saw a few masts and derricks but no sign of the *Lady Isle*. I started to think maybe she wasn't in or they had sailed without me. There was a man in a uniform who had just come out of a building. I asked him if he knew anything about the *Lady Isle*.

'Excuse me, sir, do you know where I can find the captain of the Lady Isle and is she in the harbour?'

'That lazy bastard! He'll still be in his bed, come with me,' he snarled.

I later found out that they both hated each other! He took me to the edge of the dock where this little boat was sitting, her mast and derrick just showing above the wall. I didn't know anything about high and low water then. He roared down, 'Hey, Darrach! Yer new deckhand is here.'

He told me to climb down and he threw by bag down to me. A lump came to my throat. There had been a mistake; this was not like the photographs I saw in

SS Lady Isle (I)
This is the original steam version of the puffer that became the first *Lady Isle*. She was built in 1941 as a VIC (one of the Victualling Inshore Craft commissioned by the Admiralty in World War II and based on the puffer design) at Dunstan's on the Humber. Note the fresh air position of the man at the wheel and how his view is partially obstructed by the funnel. She was bought by Irvine Shipping and Trading in 1949 but she was stranded and became a total loss in 1956. *Courtesy of the Ballast Trust*

the office in Irvine. I later found out that the photographs in the office were of the much bigger ICI ships, the *Lady Roslin* and the *Lady Helen*. What a let down!

'Is this the Lady Isle?' I asked as a cheery but not-too-clean face appeared at the galley door.

'Fit is it John? Is this oor new deckhand? Come away abaird I'll catch yer bags fir ye!' I went on board with a sad heart. This was not what I expected – Andy Samson's words ringing in my ears 'dirty wee coal boats'. The not-too-clean face introduced himself as Ernie; he was the engineer. The skipper appeared; he was John and his brother Paul was mate and with myself we made up the crew of the *Lady Isle*. With the four of us in the galley it felt a bit claustrophobic, after being used to wide open spaces but I soon got used to it. Ernie had the frying pan on and offered me a bacon butty which I wolfed down with a mug of tea with tinned milk. I was starving after my long journey. Still thinking I might be on the wrong *Lady Isle* I cautiously asked if there was a bigger vessel of the same name, as this one looked something like the *Vital Spark* in the Para Handy series, which had been broadcast on the telly. I was quickly assured there was only one *Lady Isle* except for the island that lay off the coast of Troon. The *Lady Isle*, *Spartan*, *Kaffir*, *Anzac*, and *Lascar*[3] had all been converted from steam to diesel and were the motorised version of the *Vital Spark*, the modern 'puffer'. What a shock! Oh well, in for a penny, in for a pound. I was going to give it a try. I could always get a job on a farm I thought but I was to spend the next 29 years in a love/hate relationship with the 'puffers'. Not bad for a boy from the country.

The *Lady Isle* was not loading that day so I had time to look around and was shown which bunk was mine. This was a closed-in affair which had been built from the panelling out of old railway carriages. The gap to climb through was covered with a curtain, which didn't look too clean! It did have a wee bunk light though. That afternoon the owner came on board and gave me three blankets, which I think were ex-army and made with horsehair. I also received an old pillow that his wife was throwing out! We didn't receive sheets, towels, pillowslips, soap or toilet paper in those days. The owners didn't want to spoil us by giving us too many luxuries.

Next day we were to load a cargo of coal for Rothesay, so had to move berth and go under the coaling crane. The mate Paul was on the bow. My job was to let the after ropes go and then re-run them at the coaling berth. I hadn't a clue what to do.

'Pull the rope in or it will go round the propeller, for fucksake!' The skipper screamed.

'Take it off the bits first! Right … pull it in and coil it ready to put back out. No! No! Put it through the fairlead first or you'll pull the rails off when you make it fast! Right … pass the end to the ropeman. No! No! Throw the heaving line up,

---

3 *These four were owned by Hay-Hamilton Ltd.*

you'll never throw the rope up, its too heavy! [What's a heaving line?] For fucksake where's the heaving line?'

Ernie came to the rescue. Stern rope ashore, loading starts. Calm resumes but not for long. We needed to move about six feet as the big railway wagons were a tight fit for the hatch.

'Take the turns off the bitts and let out about six feet and then hold on.' The skipper shouted. This I duly did, not knowing the engine was going ahead, instead of just slacking off I took all the turns off the bitts, the boat shot ahead with the wagon almost crashing into the wheelhouse beside the skipper. I can't repeat the curses that were uttered by the skipper. Ernie came to the rescue once again, which he did often during my first three months on board.

Everywhere was covered in coal dust: decks, wheelhouse, ropes, bollards. It was in my hair, on my face, in my clothes … what a dirty job! And it was only half past eight in the morning. Loading was soon finished and as there were no other puffers we stayed where we were in the meantime. I heard the skipper telling the mate that we would leave the lifeboat as he thought we were coming straight back for more coal after Rothesay. I didn't know what a lifeboat looked like but peering over the berth where we had been lying I saw a wooden boat. That must have been it. I didn't want to sound alarmist but I remember seeing 'Mutiny on the Bounty', when Captain Bligh and some of his crew were cast adrift in mid-ocean in a lifeboat. Were we not supposed to do something similar if we hit a reef on our way to Rothesay, or started to sink? The four of us would have to abandon ship, hoping the television cameras were in the area! Ah well, the skipper knew what he was doing. It didn't take me long to find out that the so-called lifeboat was really a bloody nuisance. It had to be lifted on and off at every port and if the weather was bad it had to be set on chocks, or usually three or four tyres, to keep the keel from tearing the canvas hatch cover. It was then lashed down to keep it from moving – a real pain in wet and windy weather.

'Right lad, go and put the breakfast on. There are sausages, bacon and eggs and I think fruit pudding in the cupboard. Smell the sausages first just in case they are off. You'll find lard in the cupboard as well. The frying pan is under the cooker, it should be clean enough. Ernie only used it yesterday. I'll help swing the derrick in, we won't need the hatches on[4], it's a nice day outside.'

So ordered the skipper, bringing me back to reality. I opened the galley door and climbed in. As the door was lower than the deck there were three wooden steps to go down. The scene that met me was terrible. There was coal dust every-where – on the table, on the cooker, sink, worktop, galley seats and floor. I couldn't handle that. Where did it all come from? I then noticed a porthole open; this was where it came from! At that the mate looked in so I moaned at him about the dust.

---

4 *Not a safe practice but putting on hatch boards was hard manual work on the puffers.*

'It's the deckhand's job to keep the galley clean and tidy and make sure the portholes are shut when we are loading. You will just have to clean it up, but don't take too long as we are wanting our breakfast before we sail.' He then slammed the door. I had to remind myself to keep calm. I gave the table a rough wipe along with the cooker and worktop and then started the breakfast. I felt a wee bit better. I got out the sausages and gave them a good smell. They seemed okay. There were about nine in the packet, seven rashers of bacon, four eggs and four slices of fruit pudding.

I gave the mate an extra sausage just in case they were slightly off, and the odd slice of bacon, which left an even number for the rest of us. As this was my first attempt at cooking I was quite pleased with the result. The mate was the first in the galley so I gave him his breakfast and watched his face as he gobbled his sausages. No ill effects. That was the first of many hard lessons I was to learn in the years to come. Breakfast finished, I washed the dishes while my hands were reasonably clean.

'Right Ernie, start up and we will get going. Right lad, let go that stern rope and the head rope and jump back on board. I'll slack off the stern, Paul will be in the bow,' were the skipper's orders. I caught on that I was to scramble ashore and throw the ropes off the bollards. We steamed slowly out of the harbour and I went back into the galley to clean the rest of the coat dust off.

'Hoi! Come out here and coil this stern rope up or somebody will trip on it … coil it beside these other ropes. That's part of your job. Don't leave loose ropes lying about the deck. They could get washed into the propeller and that would be serious,' the mate said.

'I was going to wash the dishes and clean the galley,' I replied.

'Well, always make sure the ropes are coiled first and there is nothing loose lying about, like five-gallon drums, shovels, wedges, anything that might cause an accident.' Oh aye, I thought, here we are on our way to Rothesay, no hatches on, no lifeboat with us. Oh well, the skipper knows what he is doing.

I wish I had learned to swim though.

CHAPTER 3

The First Trip

With dishes washed and galley clean, it was time to relax. Sea calm, fine and sunny, ideal.

'Is the kettle on? The skipper wants a mug of tea, two sugars and a spot of milk and I'll have the same. Bring them up to the wheelhouse,' shouted the mate through the escape hatch on the deckhead. This hatch was always left loose except in heavy weather and was right behind the wheelhouse door and so was handy for shouting down to the poor deckhand wherever tea was required. The tea in those days came in packets, one teaspoon per person and one for the pot was the rule. Here is the recipe for puffer tea:

> Bring kettle to the boil, put required amount of tea in teapot. Add boiling water, let teapot stand for two minutes. Pour into mug, adding sugar and milk to taste. A simple rule of thumb is, if you can see the bottom of the mug it is not puffer tea.

The tea was made and Ernie was in the galley so I had to make tea for four.

'How does that look, is it strong enough?' I asked, not having made tea before. I never drank tea or coffee at home, water only. It turned out the tea was fine so I made it the same way every time. We had a nice run up to Rothesay, past Ardrossan, then past Hunterston power station, Millport, where Ernie lived, and through the tans where we met the puffer *Anzac* making for Troon. A large cargo ship passed ahead of us with loads of derricks. Ernie said it was one of Donaldson's and probably bound for America. She was a regular trader to the Clyde. We then rounded Bogany Buoy and into Rothesay. Of course, I didn't know any of these names; Ernie told me. On arrival at Rothesay Ernie helped me with the ropes, as I had to jump ashore. I managed to put the ropes onto the right bollards without getting shouted at. As the skipper's future wife lived in Rothesay and Ernie was going home, Paul suggested we have a fish supper for tea. It sounded good to me. Zavaroni's was just across the road. I had never made a dinner before and was not looking forward to it.

As Paul had given the *Lady Isle* a good wash down in Troon whilst I made the breakfast, she was reasonably clean. I needed a good wash myself if we were finished for the day. I went into the galley to find Ernie at the sink and Paul, the mate, waiting his turn. John, the skipper, had a basin, which he filled first. I was to find out that there was a pecking order on the puffers for everything personal. Skippers first, engineers second, mates third and deckhands last.

'You should have emptied the garbage pail before we arrived, it'll smell the galley after a while so do it tonight after dark, but don't let anybody see you,' said the skipper as he looked round his cabin door. 'It's your job!' We kept a bucket beside the cooker for the galley rubbish; egg shells, the remains of the teapot, old bread, tattie peelings etc. I forgot to empty the garbage bucket on numerous occasions, until one day it was really full. We had just sailed from Brodick on our way back to Troon. There was quite a big swell running and *Lady Isle* took a roll and so did the garbage pail. Egg shells, tattie peelings, tea leaves, empty tins were scattered over the floor. What a mess! Another hard lesson learned. It didn't happen again.

After the skipper and engineer had gone ashore, Paul sent me over to Zavaroni's for fish suppers. I thought I'd better get three in case the mate was really hungry. He wasn't! Oh well, it was a pity to see it go to waste so I just spread another two slices of bread and used it up. And so ended my second day on the puffers and I hadn't missed the telly one bit.

The layout of the *Lady Isle* was simple. The skipper had a small cabin at the front of the housing, his door leading into the galley between the funnel and the sink; then a worktop, a small two ring cooker with a small grill, which hadn't

MV *Lady Isle* (II)
The *Lady Isle* as a diesel puffer. In comparison with the picture in Chapter 1. Note the difference in the superstructure at the aft end. The helmsman has an enclosed wheelhouse in front of the funnel. All crew accommodation was now in this area. This is the vessel that became the author's first berth. Built in 1942 at Dunstan's she was purchased in 1957 after the loss of the first *Lady Isle*. In the post-war period it was cheaper for puffer owners to buy (at a cost of £3-4,000) from the Admiralty than to build a new ship. Around 20 VICs were bought for the puffer trade by various owners.
Courtesy of the Ballast Trust

been used for years and a small oven. There was the galley table, which was just big enough for four; next to the table there was the door which led to the accommodation for the three of us – down four or five steps. There were two lockers and three drawers plus a coal stove, the funnel of which ran up to the emergency hatch and went out through the side at a slight angle; not much chance of escaping this way if the fire was lit, as the funnel got red hot. In the winter time when we turned in, the sweat would be running out of us and in the morning the frost would be sticking to our clothes. Well, maybe not quite, but unless we kept the stove banked up it could be very cold in the morning as the fire only lasted two or three hours.

There was no access from the galley to the wheelhouse or the engine room. You had to go out of the galley door on the starboard side, round the after end and down the portside to the bulkhead ladder and climb up to the wheelhouse. In heavy weather and fully loaded it was nearly impossible to leave the galley and dangerous if you opened the galley door, which I did one day just to see where we were. The *Lady Isle* dipped her stern under as a green sea swept aft, filling the accommodation and soaking myself. Another lesson learned! The toilet was about 4'x2' and was flushed by throwing a bucket on a rope over the side and filling with seawater. It was impossible to use in heavy weather. Puffer life wasn't easy.

'Are you alive down there? It's half past seven,' shouted the skipper. I climbed down from my bunk and thought 'God, but these blankets are itchy', checking my skin in case it was something else. No, nothing was crawling about. I was going to see if mum had any old sheets and a pillowcase the next time I was home. The skipper had the tea ready. Paul followed me into the galley.

'It's the deckhand's job to get up first and make the tea.' the skipper said. 'It's also your job to make out a stores list and go for stores and make sure we don't run out of anything. The company only give us about fifteen shillings a week each and it's added to our wages. We normally chip in two pounds each. That's usually enough for seven days.'

'I've got some money here, who do I give it to?' I offered.

'No, you are okay, we'll start off when we go back to Troon and load up on Thursday. I think we are for Tiree,' added the skipper. As there were no hatches to take off, the shore crane started unloading just after eight o'clock. Paul made out a stores list: bread, eight rolls, two packets of bacon, potatoes, a tin of peas.

'Get something for the night's tea' he says, as he handed me the grub tin. It had £1-18/6d in it. Food was cheap in those days. What could I get for the tea? I kept repeating to myself. Four pies, that'll do! Pies, peas and tatties. I wasn't sure how to make mince or stew as yet. It wasn't long before I was being tested. I returned from the shops. Ernie was back on board from his night at home.

'Stick the pan on lad, we'll have a couple of bacon rolls.' shouted the skipper from the wheelhouse. The frying pan was the most widely used piece of equipment on a puffer, as fry-ups were the staple diet of most puffermen. Very few of the puffers in the 60's had fridges, so it was a matter of using up what would go off first and keep what would last longest.

The discharge at Rothesay finished about half past four and we sailed back to Troon arriving about eight o'clock. The tea was a success. After tying up in Troon I reckoned we had three hours overtime and asked the skipper who kept a note of the crew's overtime and how it was paid.

'We don't get overtime for sailing, it's part of the job. We get overtime if we load or discharge cargo before eight in the morning or after five at night, or all day Saturday or Sunday. But nothing for sailing to and from ports and the rate is six shillings per hour.'

'But we have just worked a twelve-hour day, we should be paid for it, it's wrong,' I replied.

'I know Keith, but that's the way it has been for years and years. We just have to accept it or the owners will get someone else. It's the same on Hay-Hamilton and Ross & Marshall boats as well.'

Another day had ended. We knew for definite now we were loading for Tiree. The engineer had ordered fuel and oil and the waterman had been round. I had filled the two tanks with water as this was my job too and we carried about 90 gallons. In Troon there was actually a grocer who came down and took your order for stores, butcher meat, cigarettes, tobacco which was very handy. Paul made out the stores list to give me an idea how it was done.

There were one or two puffers loading first, also a small coaster called the *Isle of Harris* so it was late afternoon before we loaded. One of the owners arrived but did not come on board. The skipper went ashore. I notice the owner seemed to have a disability, but later found out that it was just the weight of his gold watch and matching ring and cufflinks that made him lean to one side! And we're not paid for sailing, eh!

Bunkers, oil and stores on board it was our turn to shift berth and load. Oh well, here goes! The ropeman let the rope go, as they were slack I forgot to take the turns off the bitts.

'Take the turns off the bitts,' shouted the skipper, 'and coil the rope up same as Tuesday, put the end through the fairlead and pass it up to the ropeman. You won't need a heaving line as it is high water, can't you see that? Right, take in the slack first. I want the front of the wheelhouse in line with that pile on the quay wall. Right! Right! That's about right. Make fast! Make fast! Take a turn.'

I couldn't get the hand of the figure of eight round the bitts and wrapped the rope round one bollard with about four turns. I was pushed out of the way by the skipper who then did it right.

'If I had gone ahead with the rope the way you had it, you would have got a nasty rope burn or trapped fingers,' he shouted and went back to the wheelhouse shaking his head. Of course there had to be four or five dockers watching; I felt demoralised and went to sit in the galley, making sure the porthole was closed.

11

The dockers started loading. Coal dust was everywhere but not in my galley. I was learning fast.

'Where are you?' shouted the skipper. 'We need to move back six feet so as to load the box.' This was a portable bulkhead we had put up about a third of the way down the hold to separate the cargo so that the coal didn't keep shifting, the nearer the floor of the hold you got. I was only two cargoes away from learning the advantage of the bulkhead and another shock about puffer life. I jumped out to move astern but Ernie had beaten me to it. Saved again. The loading was completed. What a mess! Coal and coal dust was everywhere. I watched and assisted as best I could when putting beams and fore and afters on. The two beams were put across the hold into slots welded to the side of the hold. The three fore and afters fitted into the centre of the beams and into brackets and locked everything in position. The hatch boards were laid onto the fore and afters and made a tight fit. All this was done with the ship's derrick, except the hatches, which were manhandled after being pulled out from the coal that spilled from the wagons, a very dirty job. After the hatches were placed, the locking bars were taken out from the hatch wedge cleats and any coal trapped there was cleaned out. The canvas hatch covers were then pulled evenly across and folded at the corners with the fold going along the back of the hatch at the stern and down the side at the front. The covers were then tucked in behind the cleats, the locking bars put in position and the wedges were hammered in. It was my job to finish off by putting the wedges in. We then moved to pick up our lifeboat and lashed it on deck.

'Right lad, how about the tea? What are we having?'

'I don't know,' I groaned, 'I'll think of something.'

I made for the galley, washed my hands, looked at my face in the mirror. It was the same as Tuesday; black, clothes in the same state. Oh Hell! Who cares? I looked at the time. It was twenty past five. Mum would be dishing up the dinner at this time. I wondered what they would be having. Thursday, it would be home made steak pie, boiled potatoes, vegetables followed by fruit and custard or possibly clootie dumpling. My mum was good at the clootie dumpling. Always plenty of fruit in it! Oh, well.

I peeled some tatties. We had plenty of food on board. For quickness, I fried the gigot chops with some onions. Tea finished, the dishes were washed.

Then I went for a wash ... to hell with the pecking order.

CHAPTER 4

Round the Mull

The skipper had worked out the tide for the Mull of Kintyre. We were sailing at midnight. Paul and myself were to be on first watch. What unsociable hours these guys worked, with no complaints. You had to accept it or leave. The cargo had to be delivered.

'Right lad, here is the alarm clock, set it for half past eleven. Put the kettle on and give everyone a call. We'll have a quick cup and get underway.' It was then eight o'clock. At midnight the ropes were let go, coiled and lashed and we waited to clear the harbour then dumped the garbage overboard and secured the pail. It was a fine night, if only I could have stopped yawning. Working those hours was totally alien to me and not being paid made it worse. About two o'clock the mate asked me to take the wheel so he could go to the toilet.

'Steer west by south a half south,' he told me. I had no idea what he was talking about, having never steered a puffer before.

'Is it the same as steering a tractor?' I asked him. 'I don't know anything about a compass either.'

'Okay,' he said, 'do you see that flashing light on the starboard bow? Keep the

The harbour at Scarinish on the island of Tiree, was the scene of the author's first venture to the outer islands of the Hebrides. The drying-out character of the spot, the simple stone jetty and the narrow entrance typify the difficulties of navigating to deliver cargoes to remote West Highland communities. There is no crane on the pier and this shows why the true puffer had to be self-discharging.

bow on that light until I come back. If the light goes to the port side of the mast, turn the wheel to port, okay?'

I was on my own. The minute he left, it happened. The light was on my port side. I pulled the wheel to port. This was hard work. The light was back on starboard side and going further round. I pulled the wheel back to starboard, the light was back on the port bow and going further. I pulled back to port, the light still on port side. I pulled further round, something was wrong. No, it couldn't be! The light was on my starboard bow. I tried to keep that light steady. I was doing okay or so I thought.

'Where the hell are you going?' shouted the mate who had just entered the wheelhouse.

'I'm steering for that flashing light, you told me to,' I replied.

'That's Turnberry light. You've altered course by about ninety degrees. Pladda light, the one I said to steer to, is on our starboard beam. Go and make a cup of tea and bring up a packet of biscuits.'

I sneaked quickly out of the wheelhouse in case he passed out. I would have hated to have had to give him the kiss of life. It was quarter to four.

'Go and give the skipper and engineer a shout.' Boy, was I glad to get to my bunk.

'Right Keith, that's the time,' said the engineer as he gave me a shake.

'Bloody hell, what's happening now, it's only twenty past seven,' I mumbled to myself. I staggered into my clothes still half asleep and not too happy. Ernie had the tea made.

'What's wrong?' I asked Paul. 'I don't start until eight o'clock.'

'You have to make the breakfast for the change of watch, it's the skipper that said to me to wake you up.'

This was no use. I couldn't take much more of this way of life. I had hardly had a decent wash, my clothes were filthy. I was tired. I was trying to sleep on blankets that were itchy as hell. I had been shouted at, every menial task seemed to be mine. We didn't get paid overtime for sailing through the night. No, this was not the life for me. I hated it. I was fed up. I couldn't cook. When we got back to Troon, that would be it. I would be off, I mumbled to myself as I crashed the frying pan. Sausages, bacon, black pudding, fried bread with an egg, sunny side up. I was still going to leave when we got back to Troon but kept all this to myself. Breakfast was finished, the dishes washed and the mate happy. Ernie was always happy.

We had rounded the Mull of Kintyre and were heading for the Sound of Islay. I didn't know this myself. Paul, the mate, told me when I asked him on watch. It was a fine, clear morning with good visibility, with a lazy swell running.

'There's the Paps of Jura right ahead, Islay on the port bow, Rathlin Island with Northern Ireland in the background, just abaft the beam. That is Gigha on the starboard bow and there's Machrihanish just showing round the headland.' It was all beautiful to behold and I felt a bit better. I went and made two cups of tea without being told. I was slowly getting into the tea-drinking lark. I decided to make the night's dinner, then it would be ready to heat up and the tatties boiled, ready for the change of watch at four o'clock. I had no idea about how to cook stewing steak but remembered by mother cutting it into cubes, adding carrots and onions and bringing the lot to the boil and cooking it for a while. I tried that. Result: stew, tasteless and tough; tatties, too much salt – dinner was a disaster. I thought I would stick to the frying pan! I didn't know. Was I too proud to ask the skipper or mate or Ernie to show me or tell me how to cook stew, mince, chicken, fish, etc? Or didn't they care? Did they just live in their own world or did they go through the same when they were deckhands having to learn the hard way?

I was back on watch again after my disastrous dinner. The *Lady Isle* was in the Sound of Islay. I heard John, the skipper, telling Paul we had missed the Saturday morning tide for Scarinish and would probably go to Gott Bay Pier and wait there for the next high water. I didn't know what that meant. The skipper looked a bit worried about something. I asked Ernie later on about what was worrying the skipper.

'We've missed the tide at Scarinish which means that the boat has lost a day and won't discharge until Monday and Tuesday. If we had caught the three o'clock in the morning tide we would be sailing on Monday afternoon and loading in Troon on Wednesday. It'll now be Thursday before we load. John will be pulled up for not sailing right away on Thursday night instead of leaving it until midnight. He lost four hours.'

And I was worried because I didn't cook the stew properly! The passage went smoothly through the Firth of Lorne, past Lismore, where the owner[5] of the *Lady Isle* originally came from, out through the Sound of Mull, past Coll and into Tiree. We tied up at Gott Bay Pier.

I took the mince out. There seemed a lot of it and I said so.

'Aye,' Paul said, 'there is three pounds there, if you cook it all, we can have tonight and tomorrow's dinner out of it. That way it won't go off. There is a piece of boiling beef left. If you cook it on Sunday it should keep until Monday night.'

All the meat and sausages had been put in plastic bags and placed in a bucket of salt water to keep it cool and it was then kept outside, away from the heat and sunshine. If you changed the water regularly you could keep fresh meat for a fairly long time that way. Ernie and Paul were helping me in their own quiet way.

I was just about to put the mince in the pan and fill it with water when Ernie stopped me. Paul and John had turned in.

'I'll show you how I used to make mince. A little bit of salt, simmer, add vegetables, simmer until ready, add bisto to thicken, very tasty.' With practice and

5 Captain McCorquodale at that point owned a 50% share in the Lady Isle. The other portion was owned by Irvine Shipping and Trading, a subsidiary of Ross & Marshall Ltd.

many attempts I finally managed to get it right. Here is a pufferman's recipe for puffer stew:

> Take one thick-based saucepan, drop in a large lump of butcher's dripping, melt until very hot. Cube the stewing steak and drop into the hot fat. Add a large pinch of salt, stir well until the meat is well browned, but not burned. Drain off the excess fat but leave some, as this adds to the flavour. Cover the meat with water and bring back to boiling point, lower heat and simmer until tender: about one and a half hours, depending on the quality of the meat. Add chopped vegetables such as carrots, onions and turnip (optional). When ready, thicken with Bisto, or cornflour or add Oxo cubes. Serve with new potatoes, making sure the skipper and engineer have an extra spoonful and an extra potato each. Remember the pecking order!

Tiree is a very flat island and when approaching from seaward is quite uncanny as you see the houses first on the horizon then the land. Hardly any trees or bushes grow on Tiree due to the constant sea and strong winds that blow in the winter. In the 60's and 70's all the coal was delivered during the summer months, May to September, because after September the weather started to break; the puffers couldn't reach Tiree or Coll because of the Atlantic swell. The car ferries[6] in those days had difficulty reaching the islands from September to March and quite often had to turn back to Tobermory to await a lull in the weather.

As everybody had turned in I decided to explore part of the island and went for a walk. At the top of the pier there was a man fixing creels. He spoke to me in some strange language which I didn't understand and when his dog, which was lying at the side of the road growled and bared its teeth, I caught the word 'puffer' when he called out to it. I mumbled 'hello' and carried on.

What a strange place, houses scattered here and there, no shops, no streets, just single-track roads. Didn't see any sign of people. I carried on walking, following the road. An old van passed. I stepped onto the grass, the driver waved. He seems friendly enough, I thought. I had walked for about 45 minutes and thought I had better turn back. I thought that I saw a curtain being pulled back in a house I had just passed. I was sure that a face was peering from behind a stack of peat.

'Keith, you have been too long at sea, get a grip, nobody is staring at you.' I said to myself. 'I will soon be back on board.'

There was the pier. I saw another puffer in the bay and wondered where she was bound. It looked something like the *Lady Isle*. It was the *Lady Isle*! Panic set in as I realised that they had left me stranded there. I knew my cooking was bad but I

---

6 *Caledonian MacBrayne's ferries which ran out of Oban.*

didn't want to be left. I had reached the top of the pier where the man was fixing his creels. Panic had really set in as I was waving my arms wildly and jumping about.

'If you cut across the grass here and head for that building with the flat roof you will be in time to catch their ropes as they come into harbour. I'm the coal merchant and I was expecting you at three o'clock this morning. Tell the skipper I'll have the lorries down at nine o'clock on Monday. We don't work on Sunday.'

'Thank you, thank you,' I shouted as I raced across the grass.

He had spoken to me in English and I wondered what the other strange language was. I reached the pier. Ernie was on the after-end laughing. I think he knew I would be panicking when I saw the *Lady Isle* leaving Gott Bay Pier. We moored up okay and I put the dinner on.

'Listen lad, when you go ashore, always ask when the boat is sailing. That way you won't be left. This time it was okay as I was going to get you to walk over and catch the ropes anyway, as it is sometimes hard to put a man ashore when you are springing round.'

'Okay skipper,' I replied. 'That was the coal merchant at the top of the pier, he'll have the lorries down at nine o'clock on Monday, I have to tell you.'

The tatties and mince were finished and dishes washed at six o'clock. What would I do for the rest of Saturday night? Back home I would have been heading for Dalrymple, to meet up with my mates. Probably head for Ayr, do a pub crawl, maybe head to the 'Bobby Jones', the local dance hall. I wasn't much of a dancer but we had a good laugh at times. There was a private bus company that ran buses to different villages after the 'Bobby Jones' shut. We used to arrive back in Dalrymple about one o'clock in the morning and I then had the two-mile walk back home. It wasn't too bad in summertime, if it was dry. But in the winter with the wind howling and the rain lashing down, it wasn't much fun living out in the countryside, I can tell you.

Paul came into the galley. He had his towel, soap and razor with him. I thought it must be his birthday.

'Are you going for a pint?' he said.

'Aye, okay, I'll go and look out my clean jeans while you are having a wash. Is Ernie going too?' I asked.

'I think so.'

The pub was just round the bay from Scarinish about 200 yards from the pier. It was a bit rough and ready with a stone floor, wooden seats and could have done with a lick of paint. We didn't feel out of place amongst the locals who were dressed in a variety of gear, mostly boiler suits and welly boots. Some knew Paul from previous cargoes. They all knew we were off the puffer and everybody spoke. They were really nice, friendly people. I just couldn't understand the strange language they spoke. I was told it was Gaelic. It was spoken all round most of the islands but slowly dying out as the white settlers moved in. The young folk were leaving island life and moving to Glasgow and Edinburgh.

Sunday was a quiet day. I made the breakfast about nine o'clock. As we were having two-day-old mince, I had just the boiling beef to cook and some tatties to peel. I had been on board nearly a week! Life wasn't too bad but more shocks were to come. The skipper had decided to get the *Lady Isle* ready in the afternoon. It saved us having to rise early in the morning. We lifted the lifeboat over the side, took the cover and hatch boards off and lifted out the beams and fore and afters. We had three large coal buckets which we carried on board all the time. These were used to measure out the cargo, three buckets to the ton. As very few of the islands had weighbridges, this had been the time-honoured way of measuring out and selling the coal. Most of the lorries and tractors had partitions that could be put in to separate each croft and house's coal. Six tubs (two tons) for such and such croft, three tubs for Mrs So-and-So was the usual method of delivery – straight from the boat to the customer, no stockpiling. The coal merchant would take orders throughout the year until he had enough to justify ordering a boatload – about 130 tons. And before the end of summer he would take the orders to last throughout the winter.

'Right lad, set the clock for seven, get up and put the kettle on and give everybody a call. As the boat will be on the ground, we'll have to rig the derrick so as to pull the buckets ashore until she floats. I noticed she had a slight list off the pier today,' instructs the skipper.

I had a sneaky suspicion that this would be my job. I was right! Monday morning arrived. The derrick was rigged and breakfast finished: the last of the sausages, eggs, bacon etc all used up. I had to get some bread and breakfast stuff. I had the grub money tin and we had about £2-16/- left, which should have lasted until we arrived back in Troon.

The lorries and men arrived and the discharge started. The four men only wanted to use two tubs, so the third tub was put to the side. Two men to a tub seemed sensible to me. I watched the men fill the tubs and thought that it was bloody hard work. They must have been really well paid. I didn't fancy doing it. The shovels they used were pointed, were called diggers and were necessary to dig through some of the larger lumps of coal. Some of the lumps had to be lifted in by hand. It was brutal work. Once they had reached the floor of the hold and cleared a space they could then use square shovels. When one tub was filled, the mate lifted it up on the winch and I pulled it ashore until it was above the lorry. I then made fast until the driver had tipped it. This was done by releasing two snecks on the side and the tub was then spun over releasing the coal. The driver then turned the tub back upright and put the snecks back to lock the handle in place. I then released the guy rope and because the puffer had a slight list off the pier, the derrick swung back on board. Paul then lowered the tub and the hook was transferred to the other full tub.

What actually happened on my first attempt was that I let the guy rope go instead of paying it out. The derrick and tub flew across the hold, the shovellers diving out of the way. The derrick was carrying right round against the opposite rigging and stopped suddenly. The tub was swinging madly on the end of the wire. The mate was cursing and swearing. The four shovellers were cursing at me in Gaelic. I shouted back, 'That's the fastest you'll move all day!' Poor chaps! They had 130 tons to shovel. Normal service resumed.

After pulling the tub ashore continuously until dinner time, my arms felt as if they had been pulled out of their sockets. I couldn't see me staying at this job after we returned to Troon. After dinner the *Lady Isle* was floating so the guy ropes were changed over. The vessel was given a slight list towards the pier. The full tub was slowly paid out, tipped and pulled back on board empty. This was much easier. Ernie gave me a spell to go and get stores and prepare the night's dinner. As we were down to our last tank of water, we had to keep washing to a minimum. So I gave my face and hands a quick wipe with a damp cloth and wandered up to the shop.

The shop was a prefabricated building that sold more or less everything, from a pair of boots to hacksaw blades, tins of stew to sausages. The ferry arrived Tuesday, Thursday and Saturday and on Monday afternoon there wasn't a great selection of fresh food. I managed to get two or three packets of sausages, some eggs and bacon. I spotted a loaf of bread sitting by itself and shoved it onto the counter. I thought it would have been baked in Glasgow on Friday night, travelled by van to Oban, loaded onto the ferry, taken by sea all the way to Tiree and would be used for Tuesday's breakfast. Not bad, only three and a half days old! There was no 'sell by' date in the 60's.

By late afternoon, the shovellers had reached the floor and could use the square mouthed shovels. The discharge went easier and by finishing time, about 7.30, the coal merchant reckoned there was about 70 tons left. I laughed to myself as the men left the hold. They were absolutely knackered and black with coal dust and the amount of sweat they had lost.

I wasn't laughing by the time Friday night arrived.

CHAPTER 5

Self-discharge

The discharge carried on as normal on Tuesday with the *Lady Isle* sailing on the evening tide back to Troon. Paul and myself were on the midnight to four o'clock watch and then eight to twelve. Ernie made the breakfast, I made the dinner and we arrived back in Troon about seven o'clock on Wednesday evening. Prior to sailing from Tiree the skipper had been informed that we were loading for Ardrishaig and hoped that there were no other puffers loading before us. I didn't know what he meant by wanting to load first.

As it happened the *Lascar* and *Kaffir* were ahead of us. One of the office staff arrived with our wages and mail. No mail for me anyway. The wages weren't too bad as there was a fair bit of overtime paid. 'Aye, that's okay,' I thought. With the water board there was no overtime at all.

The skipper was informed that we were coming back to Troon, after Ardrishaig, to load again on Monday for Campbeltown. Everybody seemed in a

This sequence illustrates what it was like to have to discharge a cargo manually by shovel and 'bucket'.
Here is an example of a puffer with her cargo hold full up to the hatch coamings with coal.
(This is MV *Glenfyne* lying at the pier at Talisker, Skye. She has settled on the bottom at an angle on the falling tide.) The hatch beams on which the wooden hatch boards rested can be seen.
Courtesy of the Ballast Trust

good mood and the skipper mentioned about being back on Saturday morning. It was Thursday so discharge would be finished on Friday. They must have had a crane. Oh well, no guy work for me, which was good. The grocer had been down and taken our order. I had been told just to get a couple of dinners and breakfasts as we would store up on Monday.

The *Lascar* and *Kaffir* had both loaded and sailed, the *Lascar* for Rothesay and the *Kaffir* for Brodick. We moved under the crane. I hoped I would do it right this time. We loaded with no problems. We had the portable bulkhead up and I noticed the skipper had piled the coal up away from the bulkhead. There must have been a reason for that. Loading complete, tubs and lifeboat on board.

'Let go aft, hold onto the spring Paul,' shouted the skipper.

We were on our way once again. Up past the Cumbraes, past Inchmarnock, round Skagt Mhor, into Loch Fyne and then Ardrishaig and the Crinan Canal, locking into the basin about four o'clock. We lifted the lifeboat over the side and stuck two of the tubs down the front of the portable bulkhead. Then two lorries appeared.

'I'll go and put the dinner on and peel some tatties … tatties and mince tonight,' I said to myself as I was going aft toward the galley.

'Right lad, go and help Paul get the shovels out of the foc'sle. We'll work to about seven and try and clear part of the floor. That'll make it easier for tomorrow.' said the skipper.

'Are the men on their way?' I asked.

The process of shovelling the coal into buckets has begun. Each of these metal tubs or 'buckets' hold about a ton of coal. One full tub is about to be lifted from the hold using the ship's cargo gear. There are 11 men in the picture (and another would be operating the lifting gear) so the ship's crew of five has been supplemented by some local men to speed the discharge. (Here MV *Glenfyne* is at Uig at the north end of Skye. It is likely that the cargo was for the local inhabitants, members of the Uig Coal Club.)

'No, it's a self-discharge in Ardrishaig, we get paid extra for it. Four and sixpence per ton, cash in the hand. That will be about six pounds each.'

I was not impressed. I had done a lot of shovel work with the water board, but nothing like this. Trying to dig through the lumps of coal and standing on the coal was most tiring and sore on the ankles and backs of the legs. The coal dust was everywhere. It was brutal work, and I had laughed at the men in the hold out in Tiree. Maybe that was why nobody had mentioned anything about preparing the dinner on the way to Ardrishaig, in case I walked off. Another lesson learned. They would just have to wait for their dinner. I knew why the skipper had the coal piled up aft. We only had to dig down three or four boards until we reached the floor. Piling the coal up was highly dangerous as it meant the hatches couldn't be put on if the weather changed for the worst. But if you got away with it, it made life easier for the crew when doing a self-discharge. Less digging.

I knew of a puffer that once left Ayr deep-loaded with whin chips for the council at Lamlash. As it was a lovely summer evening, they didn't put the hatch boards on. About an hour out from Ayr the Belfast to Ardrossan ferry passed at high speed ahead of the puffer, causing a deep swell. The puffer caught the swell on her port shoulder and side, causing a lump of water to enter the hold and with the roll she took, the cargo shifted, giving the puffer a very bad list. The skipper managed to hold her steady until the swell calmed down. It was a near thing. It could have been four lives lost in a matter of minutes as she could have rolled over very easily.

With a lot of hard work and no slacking we were soon on the floor. The

Here the discharge is well-advanced. This part of the hold has been emptied down to the ceiling, ie the bottom of the hold.

22

skipper was there first and, give him due respect, he certainly knew how to shovel coal. John and Paul both came from Carnlough in Northern Ireland, Paul being the older of the two brothers. As Paul was near the floor as well, the skipper chased me to go and make the dinner. They carried on to clear the floor for the morning. Ernie, the engineer, being the oldest, was working the winch and guy rope and this sometimes could be just as hard work as shovelling. The dinner was ready. The last lorry was just leaving. John reckoned we had about 90 tons left for Friday and asked the lorries to be back at six o'clock.

During dinner, John revealed the company were not to too happy with him missing the tide at Tiree on Saturday as the rival *Spartan* loaded on Wednesday for Rothesay with the cargo we should have had. That meant we would have been loading the Ardrishaig cargo on Friday and discharging on Saturday. We had won a day for ourselves, which didn't happen very often.

As I gained more experience of puffer life and did lots more self-discharges, we turned into a really good team. As John was left-handed and Paul was right-handed, I worked in the middle and could shovel left- or right-handed after a bit of practice. John worked the starboard side going aft and the port side going forward.

We turned to at 5.30 on Friday morning, had a quick cuppa and were started by six o'clock. It was a bright sunny morning. We were on the floor using three tubs, which worked like this. John hooked on his full one and we both started filling the empty one. When the first empty one returned Paul hooked his full one on. I then moved across to Paul's side, leaving John to put in the last two or three shovelfuls. When the empty one returned John took it and hooked on his full one. That way we were shovelling non-stop. We stopped for a break at nine o'clock and had bacon and sausage sandwiches. I was knackered. Paul looked the same. It was a really hot day. We were all stripped to the waist. Break over, back down into the hold. It was warm. John had asked one of the lorry drivers to bring back pies and sausage rolls for our dinner break, which was about one o'clock. Discharge continued. There was coal dust and sweat everywhere.

By late afternoon it was really warm and I started to feel dizzy and sick. I blamed the pies and breathing in all the coal dust. I went to have a drink of water and fill a couple of bottles for taking down to the hold. John and Paul had a good drink of water as well. I didn't know this at the time but we were probably suffering from dehydration, by sweating so much and not replacing the fluids. By four o'clock we had about 20 tons to go (it looked like a hundred) and should have finished about six o'clock. Then we would make our way back for Troon and home for the weekend. I had been on board for 12 days and didn't know whether to leave or stay. It had been really hard going. These puffer men were tough boys. We finished the cargo and were paid. We sailed from Ardrishaig and arrived back in Troon at 11 o'clock.

John and Ernie were leaving at seven on Saturday morning and I went with them to catch a bus for Ayr. I had all my dirty clothes and personal effects. In Ayr I caught a bus for Dalrymple and started the two-mile walk back home. What a drag it was, carrying my gear and my legs not used to all this walking, having been stuck on board for so long. I climbed the gate and walked through the field to the house where I imagined my Mum and Dad and sisters and all the estate workers were waiting to welcome me.

Some hope! My Mum and Dad were not in, just my youngest sister who greets me with, 'You're stinking, that's terrible, I thought you were going to sea. Is there no water on these boats? I am surprised they let you on the bus. What's in the bag? Put it outside. Go and have a bath.'

At that our Mum appeared. She had been up at the big house making Lord and Lady Ailsa's breakfast.

'Hi, Mum, how are you?'

'You have lost a lot of weight. Are you alright? You don't look well.'

'I am fighting fit Mum, fighting fit.'

'No son, you were fighting fit when you left home. You are under weight. Your clothes are hanging on you and your clothes are smelling something terrible. Whatever you are working at, pack it in. Your health comes first.'

'Will you wash my clothes for me? I have three pairs of jeans, shirts, socks, underwear, everything.' I asked.

'Look at the state of them. Everything is filthy. I'm not washing those. Go away,' she said. We didn't have a washing machine at home, just a big sink, a scrubbing board and a wringer.

'I'll do them,' my sister chipped in as she rubbed her thumb and finger together.

'Ten bob,' I offered.

'No, a pound.'

'Aye, okay then.'

I went to have a hot bath which nearly choked the drain when I let the water out. I had something to eat and felt very tired, so I turned in for a few hours. It was ten o'clock and I asked my sister to give me a shout about four o'clock. I didn't wake up until eight in the evening. I blamed my sister for not shouting on me but my Mum said that they couldn't get me wakened.

'You were dead to the world. I don't think you should stay on these boats, that job is not for you.'

Maybe she was right. It was Sunday night. Should I go back on the puffers or work on a farm or try and get a job in Ayr? Everything meant having this two miles walk or cycle to catch a bus before I even started work and the same at night. I thought I would try the puffers for a few more weeks and see how I liked it then. I went to pack my bag. My clothes had been washed and dried. Good old Mum and young sister. This time I took an old boiler suit and had acquired a couple of old sheets and a pillowcase.

CHAPTER 6

Other Puffers,
Puffermen and Dockers

John, Ernie and myself arrived in Troon at eight o'clock. There were three or four puffers ahead of us waiting to load, plus one very modern looking vessel with all kinds of flags showing and a real hive of activity, people coming and going. It was the *Glencloy*. This was Hay-Hamilton's new craft; a vessel of about 250 tons deadweight. What a lovely vessel she was ... nice lines, a real modern puffer with a power derrick and grab. She had been built by Scotts of Bowling and this was her first cargo. By 1966 the steam puffer had almost died out.

I think there were only about four steamers that were still trading. The *Skylight*, *Starlight*, *Stormlight*, *Moonlight* and *Mellite*.[7] The *Mellite* was based in Greenock and ran out to the American supply ships based in the Holy Loch, mostly carrying water and sometimes a few stores. With the *Glencloy* and her sister ships, *Glenfyne*, *Glenshiel* and *Glenshira*, Ross & Marshall's bigger diesels, *Dawnlight*, *Raylight*, *Polarlight*, and *Warlight* were also in the puffer trade. The small diesel puffers, like the *Lady Isle* were to last about another six or seven years and then they too would disappear. I am glad that I stayed on them. The *Lady Morven* was an ex-Admiralty VIC[8], built in 1944, and was having her tanks taken out and being converted from steam to diesel: she would be the sister ship to the *Lady Isle*. She started trading in January 1967.

In the 60's, right through to the late 70's, thousands of tons of coal were shipped to the islands, from Islay to Skye and Barra to Lewis and also to the Kintyre coastal ports and towns of Campbeltown, Carradale, Tarbert, Ardrishaig and Inveraray. Arran, Rothesay, Millport, Dunoon, Tighnabruaich were also serviced.

Somewhere, on any day of the week except Sunday, a puffer could be seen discharging cargo or sailing to her destination. It wasn't just coal that was being delivered by puffer in those days. Loose bricks, bags of cement, slates, dressed timber, bagged malting barley for the distilleries on Islay, tar for the roads, road chips, sand and gravel, lime for the farms were all part of the puffer trade.

Most of those cargoes had to be shovelled by hand just the same as coal, either by the crew or local labour. The brick cargoes were loaded in Irvine by dockers into tubs and then tipped into the hold the reverse being done at the

---

7 *All owned by the Light Shipping Co Ltd, a subsidiary of Ross & Marshall Ltd.*
8 *As was the Lady Isle.*

delivery port. The estimate for loose bricks was 3,000 equalled ten tons. Thirty-nine thousand bricks was 130 tons – a lot of handling. The cement came in half-hundredweight bags and was slung and lifted on board. The cement was then stacked into the hold and, the same as bricks, the reverse being done at the delivery port. In later years the bricks and cement came prepacked on pallets which made for a quicker load and discharge.

The bagged malting barley was a good cargo to handle. All you did was make up snotters (short lengths of half-inch rope with a loop in the middle and spliced eyes at the ends). The spliced eyes were doubled over and slipped over the lugs of the bags. These became tight when the strain was put on them. Four bags to a lift was normal. The puffer trade in the 60's and 70's was not all one way to the islands. There were regular cargoes for the return trip, though maybe not enough for every puffer, some had to return empty.

Islay was the main whisky-making island, having had many working distilleries since the 18th century. When I started there were eight distilleries either working or on reduced capacity so Islay probably had the busiest puffer trade with coal, casks and malting barley coming in, and casks of mature malt whisky going out for Glasgow. Long John Distillers, the owners of Lagavulin Distillery on the south coast of Islay, had their own puffer called the Pibroch which ran from the Broomielaw to Islay and Skye on a regular basis. She left Glasgow on a Monday and called into different piers on Islay unloading empty whisky barrels and then loading full ones to take back to the bonded warehouses in Glasgow. She sometimes called into Campbeltown to unload whisky for the maturing warehouses there.

The puffers quite often took whisky to a bonded warehouse on the Crinan Canal and also to Paisley up the River Cart. The River Cart was tidal and quite difficult to navigate, having a few twists and turns. There was also a swing bridge to pass through. To attract the bridge keeper's attention you blew the ship's whistle and if it was broken, which it sometimes was, you shouted and screamed as loud as possible and hoped he heard you and managed to stop the traffic and open the bridge before the mast struck it. It was all exciting stuff except for the skipper. This was in the days before the motorways and if you look across from the Cart viaduct today you can still see the quay wall and the old buildings.

It was the start of my third week on the puffers and I was getting the hang of the job, though still not sure how long I would stay. Ernie had taken on fuel; I had loaded fresh water and the grocer had been down for the stores list. But best of all I had acquired an old Scottish recipe book from home, detailing how to make stovies, soups, stews, etc so there was no stopping me with my two-ring cooker, small oven and grill that didn't work. I kept the tin opener handy.

The Glencloy wasn't loading that day so we were loading at one o'clock, after dinner. The Kaffir, Spartan and Lascar had all loaded and sailed. I hadn't met any of the crews until then so it was nice to meet the deckhand of the Glencloy for the first time. This skinny, plooky faced youth came on board and introduced himself.

'I'm Terry Kelly, the deckhand on the Glencloy, what's your name.'

'Keith McGinn,' I replied.

'Pleased to meet you, how long have you been on here?' he asked.

I told him and that was the start of a friendship that was to last for the next 25 years. Terry was two or three years younger than me and had joined the puffers in 1965, so was well experienced in the job having been on the *Glenfyne* before transferring to the *Glencloy*. He asked me how I came to be on the puffers, so I told him. He said he had left the school and fancied going to sea and had wandered down to the pier, saw the *Glenfyne* lying and asked if there were any jobs going and got a start. Terry was a good cook but he told me about the time he went to fry the salt herring. The skipper stopped him just in time and gave him a clip on the ear.

'You don't fry salt herring'.

When it was loading time and Terry had returned to the *Glencloy* the *Lady Isle* moved under the crane and loading started in the normal way. I had now got the hang of the ropes. The skipper had the forecast and though it was a nice day in Troon he thought it would be safer to put the hatches on as there might be a swell between Pladda and Davaar island at the mouth of Campbeltown harbour. I was no the wiser and just did as I was told. With the *Lady Isle* battened down we were under way. It takes about five hours to sail to Campbeltown so we should have arrived at 7.30. On passing the Lady Isle, (the outcrop of rock off Troon), Ernie thought I should start the tea early as there was a lazy swell running. He didn't think it would improve before we reached Davaar and went and checked with John. Yes that will be fine and can I have the tea ready in an hour's time? I managed to do this as the closer we got to Pladda, the bigger the swell became. The plates started sliding about as did the pots. Ernie put a wet cloth on the table and this stopped it all. I couldn't understand what was happening. It was the middle of June, clear sky, sunny, no wind, where was the swell coming from. Ernie tried to explain. Though there was no wind a slight depression had passed through the Irish Sea on Sunday, causing a swell which was running northwards between the Mull of Galloway and Ireland and passing into the Kilbrannan Sound. This swell would be on our beam from then until we reached Davaar.

'Once the tea is finished secure everything and the empty the garbage pail.'

I tried to look as if I understood and put everything away and emptied the garbage pail. The skipper and Ernie were right. There was a horrible swell running. The *Lady Isle* was rolling badly and I didn't feel well. I felt dizzy and wanted to be sick but nothing came up. I started sweating and shaking and went and lie down. This made me feel worse. I opened the galley door to let some air in to see if that helped but shut it quickly as I was about to get drenched. This was terrible. How long until we reached Campbeltown? Once we passed Davaar the swell died away. I mentioned this to Paul, the mate, about the bad swell and how I was feeling.

'Ach that was nothing, just a slight swell. Wait till you see a bad day,' Paul said with contempt.

We arrived in Campbeltown and tied up for the night. The coal merchant didn't like the puffers to open their hatches overnight as the Campbeltown fishermen all had coal stoves and tended to help themselves through the night. We didn't mind as a fry of fish in exchange was quite welcome. Campbeltown had their own dockers but as it was still a tub discharge I had to pull the guy rope. As Campbeltown was the last port before the Mull of Kintyre it was a safe haven for the puffers waiting for a lull in the weather before going round the Mull and heading north.

Along the West Coast of Scotland and the Western Isles most of the puffer crews were on first name terms with the locals and vice versa. You would always have someone asking for Captain Kai, or Big Geordie, Wee Johnnie, Davie Langlands, Kelly, the names are endless. If you were in the pub at night someone always had a tale to tell or a bit of gossip, either about a local we knew or a pufferman. It was all good fun and made the job worthwhile. Campbeltown was no exception, having a few worthies of its own and it was noted for its nicknames. The Ailsa Bar at one time had dozens of the locals' nicknames written onto the walls in fancy writing and it was really interesting to read, especially if you knew the people or had heard about them. How they came up with the names is a mystery: Squeebs, Tooty, Wee Bella, Kermit, Basil, Miss Piggy, Mucker, Malky, The Ghost, Ding Dong to name but a few; they were all real life characters.

D McNair & Sons were the local coal merchants. Donald Shaw was the boss and he told me this story in later years. Archie Bell (Ding Dong) drove the coal lorry doing deliveries round the doors. One morning the police telephoned Donald to ask if he could deliver two tons of coal and ten gallons of paraffin to a farm at Southend as the vet had confirmed one of the cows had died of anthrax. Donald went out to Ding Dong.

'Right Archie, load two tons of coal and ten gallons of paraffin and take it to this farm at Southend. They need it quickly, they have got a case of anthrax.'

Archie misinterpreted what Donald had told him and thought he had to receive a case of anthrax for delivering the coal in good time. On the way out of Campbeltown he stopped to pick up two of his mates.

'Listen boys, if you give me a hand to unload this coal I'll share this case of anthrax with you, whatever it is.'

One of his mates was an authority on all kinds of drink, having been arrested a few times for being drunk and incapable.

'Anthrax,' he said, 'that's a German lager, I've drank that, it's quite strong, stronger than our own.'

Archie's foot was by now pressing hard on the accelerator after hearing this good news.

'We should better try and get there first before someone beats us to it, what we'll do is this ... we'll take the case back to my house, I'll park the lorry. I'm not delivering any more coal today. We will get a couple of bottles of cheap wine and have a party.'

All three were in favour of this and in high spirits. On reaching the farm road end, the police were waiting. The two mates were thrown out, only Archie and the lorry were allowed in. It was four hours before he returned. The police had to explain to the two worthies that anthrax was a disease, not a German lager. Ding Dong never lived that down.

As Campbeltown was a safe port it was quite common for three or four puffers to be tied up alongside waiting for a slant in the weather, especially during the winter months. Naturally the pub was the meeting place. On one occasion the Royal was being used to sort the problems of the world out and heap praise on the shipowners. In other words anything and anybody was being slagged off. One skipper stood alone, when it was his turn to buy a round he also asked for two pickled eggs, which he quickly scoffed and then he asked for another two which went the same way. At that time the film Cool Hand Luke was doing the rounds in the cinemas. This was the one when Paul Newman was in a chain gang in prison and for a bet he said he could eat five dozen hard-boiled eggs.

'That's four he has eaten,' one very new deckhand whispered to the mate. 'Huh, that's nothing. I've seen that skipper eat twenty pickled eggs, no bother.'

When the next round was purchased, another two eggs appeared which the skipper swiftly devoured. He had heard the deckhand whisper to the mate. This carried on for some time and as the beer and whisky consumption increased, so did the rumours. At the final tally the figure had reached 18 eggs and a bag of crisps. I think the actual total was ten eggs, no crisps. I can tell you this, I never ate another pickled egg for over a year. It was all good fun though and relieved the pressures of a hard life.

On Wednesday afternoon the Campbeltown dockers had given me a hard time, pulling the tubs on board and swinging them ashore. Sometimes there was too much of a list on the boat towards the quay. This made it hard for me to pull the tub back. At other times there was not enough list. The full tub wouldn't go ashore. I had to walk round to the inside and pull the tub or Paul had to leave the winch and do it.

'They are doing this on purpose, because they know you are new to the puffers,' Paul remarked to me. Why were people like that? I had never done them any harm? I didn't know any of them. It was a hard enough life as it was without being awkward. What I didn't know was a lot depended on how the coal was loaded in Troon. If the wagon was not lying straight along the hatch and the wagon was tipped fairly quickly the coal shot to one side and compressed. This gave the puffer a list. You had loose coal on one side and packed coal on the other. The opposite was then done to bring the boat back. Some cranemen were good at loading and could trickle the coal in, giving an even load. This also made things easier for the dockers when it came to trimming. The bad cranemen didn't care, it wasn't their problem. It was the trimmers job to make sure the boat sailed on a level keel and upright. Their hand was still out looking for the loading allowance on completion. Five bob to the craneman, five bob to the trimmers and at the end of their shift, they jumped into their flashy cars and jeeps and sped off.

In my 29 years on the puffers I never once met a poor docker. If you had good dockers in the hold you would ask them to take an extra couple of tubs from whichever side needed it with no problem. Some would watch the way the boat was lying and do it anyway, but not my Campbeltown friends this time. On another occasion we loaded in Troon for Campbeltown on a Friday. As they didn't work at the weekend, John said we would sail on Sunday at midday.

I went home to see my folks and have my clothes washed. My mother made scones and pancakes and a lovely fruit cake for me to take back. On the Monday in Campbeltown there was half the fruit cake left. It was normal practice to give the four dockers a cup of tea at break time. I begrudged doing this, considering we had to buy the sugar and tea ourselves as did the other puffermen. This Monday I made tea for the dockers and ourselves. I cut the fruit cake and left it on the worktop beside the sink. I handed out the tea to the dockers and went to call Ernie who was in the engine room. On returning the cake was gone! Each docker had had a slice. I thought this was terrible and said to the dockers that they had no right touching the cake. It wasn't for them. It's stealing.

'If you want your fuckin' puffer discharged, shut your mouth and don't tell us what to eat and not eat,' shouted one of them. 'You shouldn't have left the cake where it was, we thought it was for us,' said another.

Liars, I thought. I never trusted a docker again and over the years I found that a lot of them looked down their noses at us. Puffermen, it seemed, were second-class.

Our orders on completion in Campbeltown were to proceed to Irvine and load loose bricks for Brodick on Thursday for discharge on Friday and Saturday. Irvine in the 60's and 70's was a busy little port, having small Danish and German coasters bringing in packaged timber for the local sawmills, mainly in the summer months, from the Baltic ports. Silver sand was also brought in by local coasters from Lochaline, a sand mine in the Sound of Mull. It was Thursday afternoon, the dockers had finished loading and the skipper said we had 132 tons of bricks on board, just over 30,000.

I had been for a few stores. The skipper said not to bother putting the hatches on as it was daylight and the weather was fine. It only took us about two-and-a-half hours to sail to Brodick. I made the dinner on the way across. Friday morning arrived. It was winch and guy work, Paul at the winch, me at the guy. The four local men were a decent bunch, quite jovial and if they saw the boat listing too far in, took some from the inside. This made pulling the tub back on board much easier. The ferry, *Glen Sannox*, came in twice a day and held us up for a while. By five o'clock the men reckoned they had over half the cargo out and knocked off for the day. The men and lorries arrived sharp on Saturday morning and had the cargo finished by early afternoon. We sailed and dropped Ernie off in Millport, where he would join us again as we were going to the Rothesay Dock, Glasgow for coal for Millport. We were going to Rothesay for Saturday night. As we were nearly in Millport I wondered if I could chance my luck there.

'Skipper, I've just a couple of tins of corned beef and some tatties left. How about if I jumped ashore and bought three fish suppers. I could then keep the tins for Sunday night's tea. I could buy some bread and bacon in Rothesay.'

'Aye, okay then, but don't be too long as we might have to shift if a ferry comes in.'

This saved me peeling tatties and having dishes to wash. I could also have a good wash on the way in to Rothesay. After the skipper and mate of course. The *Lascar* was already tied up when we arrived. She had loaded in Troon on Friday and would be discharging on Monday, so we tied up alongside her. The engineer was still on board and caught our ropes. As he already knew John and Paul he came on board and I met Davie Langlands. Davie was about one year older than me and had been on the puffers since he was 15. Starting off as a deckhand on the steam puffers, Davie works on the CalMac Ferries today and is probably the last of the steam puffermen. Over the months and years that Davie and I were on the small puffers we ran into each other a lot and had a few good laughs. Davie was brilliant at imitating Para Handy saying, 'Och if only Dougie wis here he wid tell ye himself.' Davie asked if we were going for a pint. I was, but Paul didn't go ashore much in Rothesay. It seemed he had been in a fight with a couple of the locals one night so he hadn't been ashore since. Davie and I had a great time. As Davie had been coming to Rothesay for a long time he knew a lot of the locals and I had a bit of a hangover in the morning but managed to make the breakfast which was the usual fry up. The skipper came on board at midday and we sailed for the Rothesay Dock.

CHAPTER 7

In the Clyde

The River Clyde in those days didn't have a control centre with VHF but was controlled by manned hailing stations and signals, similar to the railways. It was vital the skippers knew the signals for each dock so he would know if a vessel was leaving or moving in the dock. The hailing stations had an internal phone system and as a ship passed, would phone ahead to let the next station know the ship had passed. The station also had a loud hailer and in the dark would ask the ship to identify herself and ask where she was bound, or which dock she was bound for when proceeding upstream. The pilot or captain would reply with the relevant answers. The hailing stations that I remember in the 60's when I was deckhand were one at the start of the channel at Greenock, one at Bowling, one at the entrance to the Rothesay Dock, one at the Princes Dock and one at Queens Dock. There might have been more but I can't remember them. Most of the hailing stations, dredgers, pilot boats and hoppers were manned by Highland gentlemen with a lot of the crews coming from Skye. So if a hopper or a dredger was seen moving the Clyde someone would remark, 'Here's the Skye navy coming!'

Ernie once told me a story which I thought was very funny. Prior to joining the *Lady Isle* he had been engineer on the *Saxon*, a steam puffer that belonged to Walter Kerr of Millport that had just recently been scrapped. For 20 years, since the Second World War, the *Saxon* had basically loaded the coal for the gasworks at Rothesay and Millport so it was in the Rothesay Dock at least once every week and as demand would have it, quite often twice. They never took the gas coal anywhere else. On passing through the entrance the ritual was always the same. The man in the hailing station would shout down in a dour voice, 'Where are you from?'

'Rothesay,' Ernie or the mate would shout back. On the way out the cry was the same.

'Where are you bound?'

'Millport,' was shouted back.

This went on week in, week out for years, usually with the same person asking the same basic question and getting the same answer. One morning a general cargo ship was sailing from the Rothesay Dock, the *Saxon* was following her out. As the big ship came slowly abeam of the hailing station with the pilot on the wing of the bridge, the stationmaster shouted across, 'Morning pilot, it's a nice morning, the river is clear for you. You should have a nice run down to the

Tail of the Bank, where is the ship is bound for?'

'Morning Angus, she is bound for San Francisco,' the pilot shouted back. At that the Captain came on to the wing of the bridge.

'Morning Captain, I hear you are for San Francisco? Are you going round Cape Horn or through the Panama Canal?'

'We will be going by way of the Panama Canal, it is a lot shorter and cheaper for the ship's owners,' replied the captain. With that the ship moved into the river. Ernie had heard all this conversation. The *Saxon* moved up.

'Where are you bound?' the dour voice said.

'San for Rothesay,' Ernie shouted up.

'Don't be so bloody cheeky, I know you are for Rothesay, you never go anywhere else except Rothesay or Millport. And tell your skipper, in the last twenty years he has never once left an allowance for the poor man in the hailing station.' In those days it was customary to leave an allowance of five shillings to the

The location of this picture is not strictly in the Clyde but in the River Cart. Only those with long memories will remember Paisley as a shipbuilding centre. This picture dates from the early 1960's. The puffer SS *Moonlight* is seen here in Paisley harbour where the puffers were frequent visitors. *Moonlight* was built in 1957 at Yarwood's yard in Cheshire and was a 'Crinan' boat capable of carrying 170 tons of cargo. *Courtesy of the Ballast Trust*

craneman, same to the ropeman, same to the trimmers. But as the hailing station was isolated they didn't receive anything.

On another occasion in the Rothesay Dock the *Kaffir* had finished loading late on a winter's afternoon. It was low water and becoming dark. Charlie Marr, the skipper, had paid out to the craneman and trimmers but was now skint and in the 60's the ropemen wouldn't let the ropes go until you paid out the five bob allowance. Charlie asked the engineer for two fair-sized washers about the size of a half crown and when the ropemen came round and asked for their money, Charlie threw the washers up to near the top of the quay wall, but made sure they fell in the dock.

'Sorry boys, that was the last of my change.' Grudgingly they had to accept the fact that their 'money' was in the dock.

'Aye well you will pay us double next time,' shouted one of them.

Whether he paid them double next time, I never found out.

The estuary of the Clyde. A puffer, silhouetted at dusk, is beached at Blackwaterfoot on the island of Arran. Though it is not apparent, she sits in relative safety in the bed of a burn.

CHAPTER 8

The Pufferman's Cape Horn

We had loaded our cargo and were outward-bound for Millport, passing the hailing station, we shouted out our destination on the way past. The *Lady Isle* arrived in Millport at two o'clock and started right away. This was a tub discharge done by the gasworkers themselves. We finished on Tuesday afternoon and were bound for Irvine to load cement for Port Ellen on Islay.

We were soon back in Irvine and loading had started. Quite a few of the Troon dockers were there working on a small timber ship which had just arrived from the Baltic. They came over and spoke to John and Ernie. I was sent for stores, which was quite a long walk. The loading took all day as every bag had to be lifted onto the pallets and lifted off again and stowed in the hold. A full cargo of one 130 tons had to be handled this way. As we were going round the Mull of Kintyre, the hatch had to be battened down, the lifeboat stowed and lashed and derrick lowered. The *Lady Isle* looked very smart and seaworthy in this trim. Because of the all day loading the tide wasn't suiting us as the Irvine Bar is tidal.

'We will be leaving about midnight and should be in Islay about midday,' the skipper informed us. We sailed on time. The mate was taking the first watch and the engineer was on with him. I wondered why but didn't question it. The watches were to be five hours which was okay by me. When the skipper and myself came on we were about a mile from the Sound of Sanda. It was a nice morning with a light wind on our port side and a slight sea – nothing to worry about. Once we were in the sound the skipper asked if the dishes and pots were all secure and would I make sure the garbage pail had been emptied. I went to do this and made him a cup of tea thinking the skipper seemed a bit concerned. The weather seemed okay to me but I didn't know the Mull of Kintyre – the pufferman's Cape Horn! Once we opened up Sanda the wind was the same but the swell had increased. The *Lady Isle* was rolling slightly which gradually got worse the nearer the Mull we got. We seemed to be moving faster than normal and I said so to the skipper.

'Aye, we have the tide with us, we are probably doing about ten knots. I hope this swell doesn't get much worse. We will be okay once we are round the corner'.

We were under the high cliffs about one mile off. The water was boiling all around us and the swell was breaking green water across the hatch. The *Lady Isle* was rolling violently and looking ahead there was nothing but lumps of water

A puffer is seen approaching the Mull of Kintyre on a passage west from the Clyde estuary. The Mull of Kintyre light, seen at top right, is about 300 feet above sea level. The curious rock formation at the base of the cliff, rather like a canine head, was known colloquially as the 'dug's lugs'. On this occasion the sea looks calm but it could be very rough depending on the state of the tide and the wind strength. *Courtesy of the Ballast Trust*

being thrown in the air. The skipper muttered, 'Jesus, look at that, once we are through that wall of water we will be okay. Hope you and Paul lashed the boat down well'.

For the next five or six minutes it was hell. The boat buried itself. You couldn't see the hatch for water. She dived into a trough. I thought she was going straight down. She cork-screwed. John shouted to me to help him turn the wheel and bring her back round. She lifted herself and cleared the water off her decks and we were through the worst of it. I was shaking like a leaf. I honestly thought we were going down. The *Lady Isle* was still pitching and rolling but not as violently as two or three minutes before. The lighthouse was coming abeam. I could see calmer water ahead which was very pleasing. As the swell was subsiding I went to put the kettle on and check the galley, which surprisingly was all right, no broken dishes, etc. I asked John what caused those terrible five minutes and he explained that it was the meeting of the tides trying to squeeze through the North Channel between County Antrim and the Mull of Kintyre, which is only 11 miles wide when the flow from the Clyde meets the flow coming up the channel. The tides meet and bounce off the land and funnel through towards the Atlantic and the light westerly winds had helped to build the swell.

The tides then turned against us. Our speed was down to about four knots, so John reckoned. I made a guess and reckoned that was why John wanted to be on watch going round the Mull so he could make the decision whether to carry on or not. As the months passed I learned that a lot of skippers always came on[9] when rounding the Mull of Kintyre. As well as Kintyre, the Mull of Oa, and the Mull of Galloway were all horrendous places to be in bad weather.

It was 7.30 and we were sailing along not too badly. John switched on the radio to have a chat with any other puffers in the area and spoke to the *Lascar* which was heading towards the Mull, bound for Troon having been to Tobermory with coal. John told him what it was like but didn't glorify it. The skipper of the *Lascar* seemed happy enough as he would have the tide with him and reckoned the surge would have eased off. They blethered away for a few minutes and signed off. There were no others on. John switched off the radio and laughingly said to me, 'The *Lascar* was coming down to the Mull three or four weeks ago, she was just past Sanda and Robbie the deckhand was reading the Campbeltown Courier. He noticed in the cinema section there was a John Wayne film showing in Campbeltown that night and fancied seeing it.

'What time does it start?' Joe asked Robbie.

'Well if we turn back now we will be in Campbeltown in time for the picture house opening,' the deckhand told the skipper. 'Aye, okay then go and tell Davie and Johnnie that we are going to the pictures tonight and will sail for Port Ellen when the picture ends. If we are late arriving we will just tell the lorry drivers we broke down.' I thought this was funny.

We arrived in Port Ellen at midday but there were no lorries for us as the *Glenfyne* was in with coal for the distilleries and the *Warlight* was in with malting barley. It was winch and guy work and John warned me to keep a turn on the cleat when paying out the guy rope as we had borrowed the loading pallets from Irvine and there would be fifteen hundred weight at a time going ashore, so the boat would heel over quite severely.

We finished discharging on Saturday afternoon and sailed back for Troon to load for Lamlash. Come Monday morning I had been a month on board and was settling into puffer life quite well. That life didn't change much in the 60's and early 70's. It was the usual round of ports in the Firth of Clyde and up as far as Tobermory with quite a lot of cargoes for Islay so the Mull of Kintyre saw us a lot. It was the same for the other small puffers.

9 Took the helm.

CHAPTER 9

Nicknames

Like the Campbeltown men, the puffermen had a few nicknames for each other and some of the office staff. Curly, he was Managing Director and he didn't have a hair on his head. One skipper who had been recently reprimanded sent him a comb for his Christmas and a get-well card. Old Two Coats, he would arrive at the puffer, suit, shirt and tie, and short trench coat which were all the fashion in the 60's. He would then put on top of all this a great big overcoat which came to his ankles before coming on board. He then looked like a refugee. We would be doubled up with laughter at the sight of him. He knew how to make the puffers pay though.

One or two of the skippers had nicknames. There was Dillinger (John McDowal). John had been born in America about the same time as Dillinger was making a name for himself as a gangster. His folks moved back to Glasgow after the Second World War, so somebody nicknamed him Dillinger. If you met Dillinger once you tried to avoid him after that. He was loud and swore a lot regardless of where he was and if he had been drinking he was even worse because he suffered very badly from stomach ulcers. The puffer Dillinger was on was laid up in Greenock so he was travelling home every night. One morning he was bent double in pain. As he passed one of the other puffers the skipper said to him quite politely,

'John, if I was you I would just buy a single on the train in the morning.'

'Whit dae ye fuckin' mean?' Dillinger snarled back.

'Well, John they charge for carting you home in a box, so you would save money by not buying a return.'

Another skipper with a serious nickname was George Smith. George was an ex-east-coast fisherman and had been on the puffers for a long time. He was a decent skipper but still retained his accent. He also had a very large nose which quite often had a drip hanging from it. So someone nicknamed him Snitch. One spring when the *Lady Morven* was passing Sgat Mhor, John decided we would gather some seagulls eggs; they were supposed to be good for baking with. He and Ernie and the deckhand rowed ashore and gathered about one and a half dozen eggs. I didn't know why they did this as I couldn't bake and nobody else tried. So the eggs lay in a pail. This particular night when we arrived in Troon, Snitch's boat, the *Anzac*, was in but broken down. We saw the crew going ashore, so Ernie said to me, 'C'mon. Let's go and get some dried grass and bits of paper and make a nest behind the Anzacs' wheelhouse and put three seagulls eggs in it. It'll look as if she has been broken down for so long the seagulls have started nesting on her.' When Snitch discovered the eggs in the morning he threw them at our wheelhouse windows and never spoke to any of us for about a month.

There was another skipper on the puffers who was nicknamed The Monster. His real name was John McNiven. John was only about five feet in height and was skipper on the *Moonlight*. The *Moonlight* was actually a small coaster of about 300 tons deadweight and traded further afield than the usual puffer trade. The Monster had difficulty keeping crews as he was verbally abusive at times and had no regard for bad weather. He hardly ever bothered with forecasts and went to sea when he should have been sheltering. It caught up with him eventually.

I heard this story from an AB who had sailed with him on a small coaster prior to his puffer days. They were approaching a port in the south of England when the main engine packed in and wouldn't restart. The Monster decided he could probably sail the vessel in and ordered the crew to use one of the canvas hatch covers to rig a sail. By tying one corner to a halyard and pulling it up the mast as high as possible and spreading the corners out and tie them to the bulwarks the cover might catch the wind. Luckily the wind was blowing in the right direction and by having the crew pull the makeshift sail along the deck, they managed to catch enough wind to give steerage. This way he succeeded in sailing

An illustration of a puffer being loaded with coal by the wagon-load at the port of Ayr, as described by the author in Chapter 2. She is Hay-Hamilton's *Glenshirra*, (1953), the first diesel puffer built specifically for the puffer trade.

the coaster into port, where the port workboat put a shore rope on and got him into the berth. 'A fine piece of seamanship,' the harbourmaster said later.

Jimmy Phimster was called Faither because of his age and ability to tell stories. Then there was the Bell Ringer. When asked why he was called the Bell Ringer, Faither chipped in with, 'Have you ever followed him ashore? All you see is two ears sticking up over his back. He's like that guy in the French film, you know the guy that lived in the bell tower.'

So the name stuck. Old Faither was the ringleader and often a bad influence on us youngsters. Once up in Glasgow there was a bunch of us together and I had just had a once-every-four-months haircut; a serious short back and sides. Faither suggested we go for a drink first, before going our separate ways.

So we all adjourned to a pub across from the Central Station where the drink was soon flowing. As the pub wasn't very busy I noticed a gent standing on his own who kept looking over at us every now and again with a puzzled look on his face. His pint didn't seem to be going down very fast. Well, not the way we were throwing it back.

'Right Faither, what are you having? Give us a light Faither. What time are you coming back on Monday Faither?'

Every time we mentioned Faither the gent seemed to become more agitated until he could contain himself no longer. He shuffled up the bar and gripped Faither by the hand.

'Are these boys really your sons? I hear them calling you Faither.' He was shaking Faither's hand vigorously. 'You've got four boys to be proud of.'

'Oh aye,' Faither said, 'We've just been up to Barlinnie Prison to collect the oldest one. There you can tell by the haircut.'

And last, but not least, Hairy Face. Tommy Ferguson hadn't shaved since he had left the army and grew the beard to make himself look older, as he was quite small in stature and had a wee boy's face. He was, and still is, one of the most knowledgeable skippers on the coast today.

CHAPTER 10

Amalgamation

In October 1968 the puffer companies came together and formed Glenlight Shipping[10]. This amalgamation didn't affect us much as our ports of call were just the same and conditions didn't alter. Looking back, life on the puffers was hard.

The rumours were rife in the summer of '68 about the companies merging and forming Glenlight Shipping. There were only six of the small diesel puffers left by then; the two steam puffers *Skylight* and *Starlight* had gone. Most of the small boatmen could see the end was in sight for them, as it was becoming harder to get local men to shovel out the cargoes of coal, especially the coal clubs where the puffers only called maybe twice a year such as Croggan, Iona, Strontian, Lismore, Craignure and Jura. The discharges were being left to the crews more and more. This didn't bother John or myself as we were men in our early to late twenties and used to shovelling at Tarbert and Ardrishaig and were very fit. The skippers and most of the mates on the *Spartan*, *Kaffir*, *Anzac* and *Lascar* were all elderly men and no one could blame them for not doing self-discharge work. After sailing and steering a puffer for most of the day and through the night, four hours on, fours off, arriving at eight o'clock in the morning and jumping into the hold with a digger and a number 10 shovel, was brutally tiring.

Once the coal merchants and coal clubs had one of the bigger boats with their power derricks and grabs, they didn't want the small puffers again. The coal could be measured by grab as easily as by tub and was a quicker discharge, saving the coal merchant money on having to hire lorries for a second day. The owners also gained with a one-day discharge as the boat was available for its next cargo a lot sooner.

With the jungle telegraph beating out the rumours of a merger, amongst the bigger puffers there was a bit of jealousy and sneering. Hay-Hamilton's boats all had radars and most had washing machines, so thought they were superior to Ross & Marshall's boats, which just had the basic compass and steering wheel. In the pub it was different though.

'Have another pint, John.'

---

10 Hay-Hamilton and Ross & Marshall combined to form the new company. As a subsidiary of Ross & Marshall, Irvine Shipping and Trading became part of the new group and Lady Morven and Lady Isle became part of the combined fleet.

'Oh, thanks very much, Willie.'

'Where are you bound for John?'

'Oh, Port Ellen with coal, Willie.'

'It's very foggy outside, John.'

'Oh, that doesn't matter, we have radar, I take it you won't be sailing until the fog clears Willie. Well, I will have to go, thanks for the pint.'

John left the pub.

'Who does that bastard think he is? "We have radar." Big deal!' Willie says as he orders a large whisky to calm his nerves. After the merger all the larger boats had radars fitted.

The company owning the Ross & Marshall lighter was the Light Shipping Company and all their vessels, like the 170-ton deadweight *Raylight* of 1962, all carried the suffix 'Light' in their names. In the 1960s Hay-Hamilton Ltd. adopted the prefix 'Glen' (a Hamilton family tradition) for their new vessels, like the 240-ton deadweight *Glenfyne* of 1965. When the two puffer companies amalgamated in 1968 it seemed an easy and graceful solution to put the 'Glens' and the 'Lights' together to name the new company Glenlight Shipping Ltd.

CHAPTER 11

Mate on the 'Ladys'

Most of the long-term puffermen had started off as deckhands and worked their way up to mate, then skipper or engineer. Some of the men were ex-fishermen, mostly from the northeast coast of Scotland and were nicknamed 'North Sea Chinamen'. Irishmen were 'Bog Arabs' and anybody from the islands were 'Teuchters'. The skippers and engineers were usually very good cooks, and how they could juggle a pot of home-made soup, tatties and mince and cabbage on a two-ring cooker and have it all ready at the same time always amazed me in my early days.

By the summer of 1968, just before the amalgamation of the companies, I had become a fully fledged pufferman having been made up to mate for just over a year. Not that it made much difference as I could by then juggle four pots and pans on a two-ring cooker, I still did a lot of the cooking. My old recipe book came in handy. John and Ernie were on the *Lady Morven*, Paul had packed in and was back in Carnlough and the skipper on the *Lady Isle* was now an old fellow from Tarbert, Callum Carmichael.

Callum had only one leg having lost the other below the knee during the war, whilst mate on a coaster. It seemed a wire rope parted, whipped back and took his leg clean off as they were tying up in some port during bad weather. Callum never complained and unless he actually told you he had lost a leg it was hard to tell when you saw him walking. Callum loved his cup of tea. Not puffer tea, but the kind the council could mix for using on the roads! He loved a cup of tea before turning in at night and would make a large pot which he would reheat in the morning. Terrible stuff! The engineer said to me one night, 'Keith if you get up through the night for any reason for fucksake empty that teapot, I'll do the same if I get up. We can't drink that.'

Another time we were in the Rothesay Dock, Glasgow. I had just come back from leave. On boarding, this large suitcase was sitting outside the galley door. I thought it was strange that the office never said anything about a new engineer or skipper joining. On looking into the galley, sitting at the table was Callum and this huge Indian with a large bushy grey beard, wearing a bright yellow turban. Both were chatting away good style in Punjabi. Callum said I was the mate and right away this large case was opened to show me all kinds of shirts, etc. I am not sure to this day whether it was Callum or the Indian who sold me a shirt. I never quite worked it out. Both shook hands and spoke to each other in Punjabi or maybe it was the Gaelic. My wallet was certainly lighter. On going down to the accommodation with my gear, lying on the engineer's bunk was an identical shirt.

'Do you think they knew each other?' I said to the engineer later.

'Don't know: maybe he is a Tarbert man same as the Skipper.'

Callum told us later he had been in the army for 15 years and had been stationed out in India for a long time and had picked up the lingo from the locals. When winter set in, Callum had to go ashore as his leg gave him a lot of bother. It was a pity as he was a good skipper.

Later I was moved to the *Lady Morven*, the other ex-VIC owned by Irvine Shipping. She was a hard-run little puffer and was doing most of the self-discharges. I was mate on her along with John and Ernie and we had a few different deckhands, most of whom couldn't keep up when it came to a self-discharge. It was too dirty and tiring for them.

Just after the Snitch and seagulls eggs prank we were loading in Troon for Ardrishaig. It was the usual; Friday morning load, sail, arrive Ardrishaig and dig down to the floor ready for Saturday morning discharge. No problem! We had done it often enough in the past. This particular Friday the dockers informed us there was to be no loading until Tuesday due to a shortage of coal. When one of the owners came on board he also confirmed that.

'Yes, you are definitely coming back to Troon for coal, we have a back log of orders to clear. So if you can finish on Saturday night you can have Sunday and Monday to yourselves. The cargo is one hundred and twenty six tons this time.'

One hundred and twenty-six tons meant an extra wagon. As the weather was bad outside we had to put the hatches and covers on and with this extra wagon we had a lot more digging to do to reach the floor. So it was nearly impossible to finish on Saturday night. John ranted and raved about the extra wagon,

'Skipper if you can't finish on Saturday night, finish off on Monday. We can still have you loaded on Tuesday. But it is up to you, Sunday and Monday to yourselves,' said the manager. With that, he left. We loaded up, battened down, loaded and lashed the lifeboat and sailed. We arrived at Ardrishaig at three o'clock.

'I don't trust them, the office is up to something,' John said.

'Na!' Ernie replied, 'we are definitely going back to Troon, it will be all right.'

The deckhand and myself had taken the hatches off when we reached calmer waters in Loch Fyne and were ready to start.

'Will we try and finish on Saturday night? Then we can go to Rothesay for the weekend?' John asked. The deckhand and myself were both single, so Rothesay sounded good. Ernie could go home and John's fiancée lived there. We all agreed we would work like hell to get finished. It was hard going as it was the biggest cargo and we were trying to finish in the shortest time. The lorry drivers worked until eight o'clock and started at six in the morning. By eight o'clock we had cleared a space on the floor so the shovelling was easier. Digging through house coal was slow work. We thought we had about 100 tons left for Saturday; it wasn't looking good. Allowing for two half-hours off and a one-hour break for dinner and finishing at seven o'clock we had to shovel, on average, nine tons per hour. Could we do this with three men? The canal manager came on board at lunchtime.

'Do you think you will finish skipper? I need to let the lock keeper know so he can let you out.'

John thought we would but it would be late, maybe nearer to eight o'clock. The lock keeper got overtime and a bung from the company for opening the locks after hours so he didn't mind waiting.

'It's not often we see the canal manager on a Saturday, the lock keepers usually keep in touch themselves. That's strange,' John remarked. We managed to finish by seven o'clock; it was the hardest cargo I had ever shifted. The dig down from the top really killed you. Never mind, we had Sunday and Monday free and cargo money and wages in my pocket – I was really flush. A long lie on Sunday, a few beers, a fish supper out of Zavaroni's … what more could a pufferman ask for? Everybody, though tired, was in a good mood. We were in the sea lock and waiting for it to run down. The canal manager came across. 'Skipper can you give your boss a ring at home, I think he wants to know if you finished alright.'

John went ashore to phone. I carried on preparing the dinner. The deckhand was watching the ropes as the boat dropped in the lock. Then I heard a raised voice.

'No, I'm packing in, the dirty bastards! This isn't good enough. They told us we were going back to Troon. They can't do this!'

I went out on deck. Ernie was doing the shouting. John was on the quay wall. The deckhand was in the wheelhouse.

'What's wrong?' I asked. 'I've just been told by old "Two Coats" to make for Glenarm and load a cargo of lime for Brodick and can I be there for tomorrow morning?' said John. 'After all our hard work, they do this to us.'

The SS *Lady Morven*. The author served as mate on the diesel-driven version. She too, had been a VIC, built at Dunstan's on the Humber in 1944. Here she is on the Clyde and is passing one of Alfred Holt's 'Blue Flue' ships, outward-bound for foreign parts. *Courtesy of the Ballast Trust*

Ernie was for packing in. John was nearly in tears. I didn't know what to say. I was single, so was the deckhand. It was a pretty dirty trick to play on us after promising Sunday and Monday to ourselves, if we finished. They knew John would try and finish and adding the extra wagon was really cruel. We normally took about 110 or 112 tons to Ardrishaig which gave us about 80 tons for Saturday, depending when we arrived on Friday afternoon. Ernie and John calmed down, we left the sea lock and tied alongside the main pier. We had our dinner and washed and turned in. John had told the boss we were too tired to sail through the night to Northern Ireland and also the hold had to be cleaned.

We sailed on Sunday morning and arrived in Glenarm at four o'clock. John went home to Carnlough to see his folks. The loading in Glenarm was done by a chute, which was hung on the end of the derrick. This was another dirty cargo to load as the lime dust blew everywhere. The boat was white for weeks and no matter how often you hosed down, the paintwork always dried white. The companies had a very bad habit of sending the boat for lime after a dry-docking when the boat was nicely painted. We often thought they didn't want their boats looking smart. John was back from his night at home and was speaking to the loaders.

'No, no, skipper, you would not have been loaded here on Sunday. They won't pay the overtime and we already work six days a week. Who wants to work on Sunday?'

So why did the boss say this about wanting to load on Sunday? The *Lady Morven* was already being run hard by a good skipper and crew. He knew we had extra tonnage on board and would struggle to finish on Saturday night and would be tired. It didn't matter. As the years passed I learned that to ship owners, cash is king. Captains, skippers, crews didn't matter as long as the boat showed a profit. Nothing has changed.

By four o'clock we were loaded, hatched up and ready to sail. Everywhere was white with lime dust. I had the deck washed, and would hose down once we had cleared Glenarm harbour. Brodick was a shovel discharge, same as coal, but only two men in the hold, the same two men who were part of the brick squad. They asked the skipper if one of the crew would give them a hand. No way! As the *Lady Morven* had slewing gear, it was only myself who was required to work the winch. It took two full days to finish the cargo. The *Lady Morven* didn't load until Thursday. As the freight rate on lime wasn't very good, the company were moaning to John about not finishing in one day and why hadn't I and the deckhand not gone down into the hold and given the men a hand. Aye right. Did the office think we were daft?

We loaded quite a few cargoes of lime but only took it to ports where there was a shore crane that could finish us in one day. The more modern puffers with their power derricks and grabs and bigger tonnages went to Brodick and to the other islands with no cranes.

CHAPTER 12
Unchartered Waters

We loaded out of Troon for a place called Croggan on the Isle of Mull, a small pier in Loch Spelve. The entrance to the loch is in the Firth of Lorne and is very narrow. There are rocks on the shore that are painted white to keep you clear of a bad rock that lies in the channel. You line up the two white rocks and steam towards them until you line up another two white painted rocks astern of you. You then haul hard to port, keeping the two painted rocks astern of you in line. As you pass the dangerous underwater rock there is a white cross marked on the shore showing where it lies. If you have done everything right you don't hit it. The puffermen never hit it. We arrived in Croggan about four o'clock in the morning having sailed from Troon at one o'clock the previous afternoon, having caught the tide at the Mull of Kintyre.

Croggan was indeed literally just a pier with a couple of houses. The telephone box sat in the middle of a field. You had to cross over a style and walk through the grass to reach it. It was very peaceful and quiet with just a few sheep grazing on the hills and a few sea birds squawking; the sun was just breaking over the tops of the surrounding hills. It reminded me of home with its quietness. We had started to open the hatches on the way in and had the boat ready for discharging. It was another full cargo. It had been a long day and night as we had been 15 hours on passage. We all turned in for a few hours. Just after eight o'clock the coal merchant arrived with an assortment of tractors and trailers and a couple of small lorries.

'Will the crew discharge the cargo? I can't get men who are willing to shovel coal nowadays,' the coal merchant asked. We were not keen, having just spent the night at sea and nobody in the office had said it might be a self-discharge. John asked for ten shillings a ton, cash. No cheques. The merchant readily agreed, provided we kept the tubs small. That way he would get a few extra tons out of the cargo, which would pay for the discharge. The coal was delivered the same way as at Tiree – three tubs to the ton straight from the boat to the customer. We worked late on Friday night and finished on Saturday evening. This was another difficult discharge as we were quite often waiting for the tractors to appear and when one did, he took three or four and a half tubs – 30 hundred weight. Then we were waiting again and at the speed we could shovel at, it was very slow and frustrating.

Lady Morven loaded coal for Iona. This was a once-a-year cargo for the coal club and it was beach work. The beach procedure was that the boat went on at high water on the first tide and dried out on the beach. The tractors and trailers came down once the tide had gone back far enough and started unloading, measuring out the cargo in the time-honoured fashion, three tubs to the ton. Once the tide started flooding and the boat began to float we pulled off and went to anchor waiting until about one-and-a-half hours after high water, depending on the state of the tide and whether it was coming near spring tides or after. As the boat became lighter, the secret was not to become neaped. You had to wait until the tide receded before beaching on the second and third tides.

That was my first time doing beach work at Iona but I had asked the skipper of the *Glenfyne* where the beach was whilst we were laying the cable in the sound. He pointed it out to me, 'Martyr's Bay it is called and do you see the telephone pole on the roadside? Well, steer straight in keeping the pole on your port shoulder until she grounds and just keep your engine ticking over until she settles on the bottom. Don't do what I did one time. I got the tide wrong and went in until we grounded, stopped the engine and turned in. The tide made another 18 inches. We swung broadside on, luckily the coal merchant saw us and came down with his boat and pulled our stern round and held us until we settled on the bottom. The other thing you don't want is an onshore breeze blowing across the sound as this can push you broadside on as well.'

I observed all the skipper had told me and as I had stayed on the helm when going through the Torran Rocks felt quite confident about going to Iona. The *Lady Morven* was loaded and I decided to sail at midnight so as to catch high water at the Mull of Kintyre and go as far as Colonsay that night. I had worked it out that high water at Iona was about nine o'clock in the morning and had decided to leave Colonsay in time to catch the morning tide. Everything went as planned.

Portrush in Northern Ireland was a busy wee port with a lot of puffer trade and the *Dawnlight* was a regular trader there. A lot of bricks, sand, gravel blocks and road chippings were loaded in Portrush for the Outer Hebrides. Quite often two boats would be in at the same time, one loading blocks, one loading sand or gravel. The loaded boats could only cross the bar at high water and if there was any swell we quite often bounced off the bottom. Very scary stuff, because if we lost steerage the ship's head would swing towards the shore which was very shallow and we were in big trouble. Tommy the harbourmaster was very good and knew the bar like the back of his hand and always told us what to do.

'Steer for the house on the far shore with the two dormer windows and when your wheelhouse comes abeam of the perch on the south breakwater, haul hard a' starboard, wheel hard over and go full ahead. Don't stop even if she bumps. Keep going and you will soon be in deep water.'

I always listened to what he told me but it was very hard not to pull back on the throttle when she hit the bottom and stopped for a brief second in the swell and then shot ahead again. I always imagined the propeller being damaged but it never happened.

CHAPTER 13

Islay: the Whisky Island

The *Lady Isle* was to proceed to Troon to load for Islay and the *Spartan* was headed for Troon as well.

'We will have to try and beat him to Troon so we can load first,' John said to Ernie.

'Okay, John. I'll give you a few more revs and we should do it.'

As house coal was about all the same quality and plenty of it being shipped, it was usually loaded first. This made a great difference when we loaded for Ardrishaig or Tarbert as we gained about an hour and was the same for catching the tide on the Mull of Kintyre. 'First loaded, first away'. As we were for Port Ellen on Islay it was to our advantage to sail as soon as possible as we would be in Port Ellen by ten o'clock at night and ready for discharge in the morning. Everything went to plan. We loaded and sailed and arrived in Port Ellen on schedule.

I had been coming to Port Ellen for over two years and knew a lot of the locals who usually discharged the puffers. A fine bunch of worthies, all with nicknames. Philco and his twin brothers, Paramore, Sean O'Leary, Chippy and a few more whose names I forget. Morning came bright and sunny. The trimmers arrived to discharge the cargo. Philco, Paramore and the twins; three pairs of welly boots, one pair of farmers' boots and six cans of beer. A motley bunch if ever I saw one.

'Morning McGinn, you're back to see us again.'

'Aye, Philco, you are looking fresh this morning. I can see you had an early night last night.'

All four looked as rough as a badger's coat. They looked at the coal, glanced at the shovels and tubs and decided to have a can of beer each. It was ten past eight in the morning.

'How much have you on board, Keith?' asked Paramore. He told me the *Glencloy* was in with barley and before that the *Polarlight* had also been in with coal for a distillery. They were a good, friendly people on Islay and as I had been coming to the island for quite a while I knew most of the gang of trimmers by name. We always had a laugh and a joke. Willie Currie was there with his two lorries waiting to haul the coal away. Willie had been in business for himself for about two years and worked really hard, seven days a week delivering coal, sand, gravel and mash from the distilleries. I have known Willie for 38 years now and met him recently in Port Ellen and although retired still drives a lorry, seven days a week.

Philco and the men started the discharge and it was not long before the whisky and beer started to flow through the pores of their skin; they were continually wiping their faces but they dug away steadily and soon asked for a couple of bottles of water. They stopped for the usual morning break and by dinner time had reached the floor of the hold when they stopped for an hour. By mid-afternoon someone had produced a half-bottle of whisky, along with the rest of the cans they had brought.

'Hey McGinn! Are you wanting a dram? Here's a can.'

'Aye, okay. Why not?'

The half bottle was passed up to me, I took a quick gulp; the can went down well after it. The discharge went well, with about 80 tons left for the next day. This wasn't too bad; 50 tons out in about seven hours shovelling with four men. We would have hoped to have had about 60 tons out in the same time with three men in the hold using three tubs. But then again, the *Lady Morven* was always being

A cask of malt whisky is being prepared for loading into the hold of a puffer at the Coal Ila distillery on Islay. The wooden hatch boards lie between the hatch coaming and the bulwark. The ship's lifeboat has been put ashore.

pushed. That's why we got so many self-discharges. I went ashore to the Islay Hotel for a pint or two and met Philco and company. A bad mistake! I had a king size hangover the next morning. They finished the cargo by late afternoon after a few more cans and half bottles had been drunk. I vowed never to drink again after the previous night … famous last words!

'See you next time McGinn,' Philco shouted as he staggered up the pier.

'I'm never coming back. I was a good-living person until I met you lot!' I shouted back.

'Aye, you'll be back McGinn. You're a fully fledged pufferman.'

On another occasion I was back in Port Ellen with coal. The coal wasn't for Port Ellen but as there was a coaster at the pier where we should have been, the coal merchant agreed to discharge us at Port Ellen and haul it round by road. On arriving early we opened the hatches ready for a start the next morning. That night in the pub we met the usual gang: Robin, Sean, Wee Bruce, Philco and Nasser. They already knew the coal wasn't for there and weren't involved in the discharge. After having a couple of very small sherries I think I went on board and turned in.

About three o'clock in the morning I woke up to go to the toilet and have a drink of water. I happened to look out the porthole and it was like a scene from the film 'Paint Your Wagon'. There were four men filling coal into an assortment of bags, two men lifting them onto the pier and two men stacking them onto a pick-up truck. Outrageous! Blatant thievery! They should have been jailed! How dare they come onboard a puffer and steal! I decided to phone the police after we finished the discharge. Oh well, it was too early for me. I hoped they would leave some for the coal merchant. The coal merchant arrived with his lorry and men and had hired Willie Currie's two lorries.

'Was there anybody on board here last night skipper, unloading coal. The boat doesn't look full,' asked the coal merchant.

'No, no,' I replied. 'I would have heard them, I am a very light sleeper.'

He was very suspicious. I hoped there was no fresh coal lying on the pier. John had phoned and been given his orders. From Port Ellen we were to proceed to Greenock to go on hire to the Americans in the Holy Loch and after that the *Lady Morven* was possibly for the dry dock, for her two-year survey, which was overdue.

CHAPTER 14

'The Yanks'

The American Navy had a supply ship that came in once per month for about three or four days to bring supplies for their nuclear submarine base in the Holy Loch. They usually hired four or five of the puffers to offload the supplies, which were then taken to Fort Matilda Pier at Greenock. Cap-I-C, as the Americans called this, which meant Captain In Charge. The usual supply ship that came in was the United States Naval Supply Ship (USNSS), *Victoria*. In the Holy Loch the Yanks had a large dry dock, which could take their nuclear submarines in for servicing. When you saw one of those submarines in the dry dock, you realised how massive they really were; fearsome dealers in death.

Astern of the dry dock the mother ship USS *Simon Lake* was moored with her stern against a large storage barge from which the small launches departed. The *Simon Lake*, barge and dry dock were all linked together by large gangways. The bow of the *Simon Lake* was anchored by double chains to a large mooring buoy; the same at her stern. The way she was moored, should an emergency have occurred, she could have slipped her moorings and been at sea in 20 minutes, or so I was told. There were also three American tugs in the Holy Loch, the *Saugus*, *Nattick* and *Piqua* and two of them were always on 24-hour standby. This was at the height of the cold war.

When working with the Americans the money was good as we were paid 15 hours overtime each day from five o'clock at night until eight in the morning. We very seldom worked all night, sometimes to about eleven o'clock and then the Americans would knock off. If we were really lucky they would keep a puffer on standby and we would do nothing while the rest of the puffers would be working their butts off.

The American jobs became regular work for the puffers over the next 25 years as the Americans moved from Cap-I-C to the MOD base at Fairlie which was further from the Holy Loch and they needed more boats. After the USNSS had sailed, quite often the Americans would keep a puffer on hire, along with the permanent boat, the *Anzac* (the *Mellite* had been scrapped by this time) to clear the backlog of stores and help at Cap-I-C.

On this occasion the *Lady Isle* was being used. The skipper was given instruction to go alongside the submarine on the starboard side of the *Simon Lake* and they would take the lifts off with the heavy lift crane on the *Simon Lake*. The

MV *Spartan* is beached at Martyr's Bay on the island of Iona; tractors and trailers are lined up to take her cargo off. *Spartan* was one of the few VICs built in Scotland. She was launched at Hay's yard at Kirkintilloch on the Forth & Clyde Canal in 1942 as VIC 18 and was bought in by them in 1947. She was converted to diesel propulsion by Hays in 1961 and it is in that form that she is seen here. She ended her commercial life stationed on the Clyde making transhipments to the US nuclear submarine base on the Holy Loch. After that she was purchased for £1 by what became the Scottish Maritime Museum and can still be seen today at their base at Irvine, in North Ayrshire. She has been placed on the 'designated list' as a ship of historic importance by the National Historic Ships Committee.

skipper eased alongside the submarine and just bumped gently. I threw a rope onto the sub, hoping one of the sailors would put it onto a bollard. Nobody made a move except the two sailors on the gangway watch – both pulled revolvers. One walked along the deck and pointed it straight at me, his colleague covered the skipper and engineer. The skipper tried to explain that we had been told to come alongside as we had some lifts for the mother ship.

'That's okay guy, you haven't got permission to come alongside the tender. Stand off until we call you to come alongside. Next time come within calling distance and ask permission to berth. We will then contact our control centre and ask for clearance. Now clear off until we call you,' one of the armed sailors demanded. Two hours later permission was granted. It was scary stuff, having a gun pointed at you.

The Americans at the Holy Loch were terrible for getting their information wrong. If there were to be four or five puffers on hire, the skippers would be told by our office on a Friday night.

'Right you have to be in Greenock on standby at zero eight hundred on Sunday morning.'

Of course, anybody who maybe managed a night at home had to come back on Saturday night as the trains and buses gave a pretty poor service on Sunday morning. The Americans were supposed to come to the Victoria Harbour and give us our orders. By midday we quite often had heard nothing so somebody would phone Cap-I-C to see what was going on, only to be told the USNSS was due at midnight and they would be in touch. Puffermen being a sociable crowd and with the pubs being open from 12.30 to 2.30, we all headed for light refreshments. Midnight would come and go with no word of the USNSS. Monday morning would arrive. The Americans would appear and tell us to be in the Holy Loch for 1400 hours as the USNSS was due then; we all could have had Saturday night and Sunday at home. This happened regularly. One day one skipper, who hated the Holy Loch job, remarked, 'They have just been to the moon and back. They can send a spaceship two hundred and fifty thousand miles to land a man on the moon, telling the world the exact minute Neil Armstrong will step on the surface. They can bring him back from outer space and give you the exact position and the time he will land in the Pacific, and yet they can't send a supply ship three thousand miles across the Atlantic and tell you which day it will arrive. It makes you wonder!'

'Aye, you're right skipper, if it hadn't been for John Wayne and Errol Flynn, they wouldn't have won anything during the war,' a deckhand chipped in. We scratched our heads and tried to work that one out.

There were two other puffers that belonged to a Greenock firm, the *Toward Lass* and *Cloch Lass*. They worked the Holy Loch taking the garbage from the mother ship and dry dock. Everything was thrown into the skips. The puffer crews salvaged anything that was saleable; boots, shoes, jackets, boiler suits, etc. A lot of the stuff was slightly soiled but was good enough for working in. Most of the puffermen in the 60's and 70's were going about dressed like American sailors; some even spoke like Americans. Three days working for the Yanks, once a month, and it was hard to tell if they came from Wyoming or Wemyss Bay. One American officer once said to a skipper, 'Gee, Christ man! Some of you puffermen are better dressed than I am and I have been twenty five years in the navy.'

I bought some gear myself at times, mostly boiler suits, which were all good quality and lasted a long time. This particular time I was badly needing a new pair of working boots but begrudged the money, so bought this almost new pair of steel-toecapped Yankee ones. They were a bit too big for me but this didn't matter; I just put on two pair of socks. I was really proud of my new boots and being almost new, looked very smart. I have to say, my feet were continually sweating and itchy every time I wore them and blamed the extra pair of socks. I mentioned this to the skipper, who told me never to wear other people's boots or shoes as this could cause all kinds of foot problems. If the Yank that wore them first had sweaty feet you would get them. I went and bought a bottle of Dettol and emptied it into them and also sterilised my feet, which helped. After paying ten bob for them and the price of a bottle of Dettol, no way was I throwing them out. I wore them for months but never again bought second-hand boots.

During our monthly visits to the Americans we quite often met the same men two or three times. Some were really friendly and would chat away to us and tell us their plans when they left the navy. Some were learning trades whilst doing their three years of national service. Some were going to stay on long term. One sailor we got to know had signed on for six years. He told us he had dropped out of college and joined the navy so he could save some money. He wanted to buy his own truck and do coast-to-coast driving when he finished his navy days. He showed us photos of some trucks, one of which he fancied buying. They were very impressive and far bigger than our own. He was telling us that his old man and elder brother both owned their own trucks and his mother ran the business; it was his ambition to buy his own truck and join the family firm. I often wonder how he got on.

On one of our visits to the Holy Loch we were the last puffer there. The rest had finished and gone elsewhere. We had this one heavy lift to pick up from number two hold to go to Cap-I-C. One of the USNSS crew came on board to help us steady the lift and take the slings off. He was a huge coloured man and smoked a huge cigar. He was looking down into our engine room when his colleague shouted, 'Hey, you Lou, what dey got down dere man?'

'Deys got a little Singer sewing machine engine Al. Ah could nearly put it in ma pocket. Ho! Ho! Ho!'

Of course, it wasn't as small as that. But for Lou, coming off an 8,000-ton ship with five hatches and about 16 derricks, it was small. We picked up the lift and returned to the harbour as instructed and went down to Cap-I-C the next day. The crane there was too small to take the lift so we took it back to the Holy Loch where they took it off at the dry dock. That was our hire finished for that month. We got an extra day, which gave ourselves an extra 15 hours overtime each; easier money than shovelling coal.

The *Lady Morven* finished her stint in the Holy Loch and was for the dry dock at Troon. I had to go back to the *Lady Isle*.

CHAPTER 15

Explosives, Anchors and Barrels of Tar

The *Lady Isle* was at the ICI[11] wharf at Irvine loading explosives for Carrickfergus in Northern Ireland; this was a run the puffers did quite regularly. The other run the puffers did from the ICI was transhipments to the Tail of the Bank. We quite often had to go to anchor and wait until the big ship had finished discharging and reloading in Glasgow before arriving at the Tail of the Bank to load the explosives. On departure from Irvine we would be told the vessel would be finished loading at such and such a time and would be at anchor when we arrived. All quite straightforward, you would have thought.

It never worked out that way. Either the dockers hadn't finished, or her cargo was late arriving. We would go to anchor and wait not knowing what was happening. As communications were bad (we had no VHF radios) and as we had explosives on board we weren't allowed to go in anywhere and telephone. However we did, and told anybody who asked, we had machinery on board that was going to the States. Sometimes when we telephoned the company would tell us to phone back later. They would try to contact the agents, who would contact the stevedores, who would try and get an answer from the dockers about when the ship would finish and be at the Tail of the Bank. Sometimes we went back to anchor no wiser than when we had first asked when the ship was due.

Anchoring on a puffer was a bit of a nightmare and took a little time. Most anchors were of the kedge type. The stock being folded when not in use. This had to be rigged before lifting overboard. Most puffers had an anchor davit with a four fold purchase, with a hook, which was hooked into a shackle at the bottom of the shank. The mate and deckhand heaved up by hand the anchor until it was clear of the bulwarks, made fast and swung the anchor overboard. A fairly short rope was then fed through the joining shackle, one end being made fast. The other end being made fast on a cleat with a few figure-of-eight turns. The davit tackle was then slackened off until the anchor was hanging on the short rope. It was then the deckhand's job to climb over the bulwarks and down the anchor and let go the davit hook, which was brought back on board. As the anchor chain was already fed through the hawse pipe and led over the bulwarks, it was only a matter of slacking off the figure-of-eight turns and hoping the short rope wouldn't jam

11 *Imperial Chemical Industries.*

when the skipper shouted, 'Let go!'

The shops in Irvine were quite far from the pier so I nipped ashore and bought a few groceries to see us through to arrival in Carrickfergus. In the butcher's shop I went to, the butcher's boy who served me that day in 1966 lives about three doors away from me just now and still remembers my first time coming into the shop. I wonder why? Of course, there is no shop there now. A shopping centre and flats have all been built in the area. The Magnum Leisure Centre and Beach Park have replaced all the railway sidings at the harbour and Irvine harbour has been closed for years to commercial traffic, as has the ICI wharf. The old tug, the *Garnock*, which used to assist the coasters alongside the wharf is now part of the Scottish Maritime Museum. The *Spartan* is also there. Living locally I see the *Spartan* quite regularly when I am in Irvine and have quite a few good memories of her.

After the *Lady Isle* was sold in 1972, I was sent to different puffers whenever they were a man short. So jumped about quite a bit. The *Spartan* was mainly trading in the Clyde at that time, eg Ayr-Millport, Ayr-Rothesay, up the Clyde, on hire to the US Navy in the Holy Loch and so only carried two of a crew.

Some time later the company had a cargo of barrels of tar that had to be shipped from Ardrossan to Stornoway and as there were none of the bigger puffers available, the *Spartan* was given the cargo and I went as skipper on her. This was in December 1973. John McGinty was the skipper in the Clyde but was quite happy to go as mate for the trip. (He was still paid a skipper's wage.) Charlie Cornish was the engineer. (He later became famous for the lobster feast in Campbeltown.) As there was only to be the three of us on board for the trip, the company were quite happy for us to stopover at night. The main thing was removing the cargo from the pier as this was costing them money.

I joined at nine o'clock on Saturday morning. John and Charlie had everything ready for sea. So we sailed right away, caught the tide on the Mull of Kintyre and arrived at Craighouse, Jura at nine o'clock that night and sailed again at seven o'clock on Sunday morning. The weather that morning was not too bad; the forecast for later on was southwest, force 4-5, so I hoped we could be round Ardnamurchan and into the Sound of Sleat before it became too rough. It didn't work out that way as by the time we reached the Sound of Mull the weather had freshened. So it was Tobermory for us and the Mishnish Hotel for orders and any gossip.

As the weather was to improve again on Monday I looked up the tide for Kylerhea and reckoned that sailing at five o'clock in the morning would suit, providing the weather was okay. As luck would have it there was only a slight to moderate swell running and as the *Spartan* wasn't deep-loaded she could handle this okay. The main problem with the small puffers was trying to steer them in a straight line especially in a following sea in the dark. There were no radars on these old puffers. Everything centred round the magnetic compass and the ability of the skipper and mate to steer by it and to try and judge how much leeway the boat was making. If the skipper or mate could see a lighthouse flashing it gave them something to steer for. In drizzle or rain and fog, with a swell running, trying to steer a straight course was a nightmare.

Most puffer skippers kept a compass course book and logged the courses in good visibility. For example, going from Ayr harbour entrance to Brodick on Arran, the skipper would line up the mast on Goat Fell, write down the compass course, check the course on the old, torn, coffee-stained chart and compare the two. The skipper would also log the time he passed Ayr breakwater and take the time he arrived off Brodick. Knowing the distance from the chart and the time it took, he could work out the puffer's average speed.

One old skipper I sailed with had a scrap log that he had kept for years with courses, time and distance, tide directions, spring and neap rates. After a few weeks on the *Lady Isle* he would sail in the poorest visibility with complete confidence in his own ability and trust in the compass. There were not as many rules and regulations in those days. Very few of the small puffers kept well-documented log books, just scrap logs for their own benefit.

The *Spartan* made a good passage through Kylerhea past Kyle of Lochalsh on up the Sound of Raasay and we arrived about eight o'clock on the Monday night in Stornoway. The *Spartan* discharged her cargo on the Tuesday and loaded empty tar barrels on Wednesday to go back for Ardrossan. We sailed on Thursday morning, stopped over in Tobermory, sailed on Friday morning and arrived back in Ardrossan on Saturday morning.

Although I was not the last skipper to sail on her, *Spartan* never went round the Mull of Kintyre again or through the canal to anywhere in the Western Isles. She ended her trading days in the Clyde and eventually finished her days on hire to the Americans based in the Holy Loch, before arriving at the Maritime Museum[12] in Irvine.

12 Glenlight Shipping sold her for £1 to the West of Scotland Boat Museum who then transferred her to the Scottish Maritime Museum at Irvine, where she can still be seen.

CHAPTER 16

Skipper of the Lady Isle

John left the puffers and became a pilot at Irvine for the ICI. I was still on the Lady Isle when she went on hire to Wm Press & Sons in January 1969. Wm Press had a contract to lay a pipeline for the ICI for their nylon plant at Ardeer in Irvine Bay. I was to remain on this job until its completion one year later and by the middle of the summer was made up to full-time skipper.

When the pipeline job finished in January 1970 the Lady Isle started trading again, after dry-docking in Bowling to have her bottom cleaned and painted and her engine overhauled. By this time Troon was closed and all the puffers traded from Ayr. Ayr was not a good move for the puffermen as the dockers worked double shifts, six until three, three until midnight. Quite often we could finish in Rothesay in late afternoon, sail to Ayr, load and be back in Rothesay for the next morning. This also happened for other ports as well. The working week for the puffermen had increased to an average of 80 hours.

If you worked it out that the discharge in Rothesay started at eight in the morning and completed at four o'clock and we sailed right away, we arrived in Ayr at about 8.15 at night. We loaded right away, which took about an hour, and sailed right away again without putting the hatches on and we arrived back in Rothesay about two o'clock in the morning. As the puffers were reduced to three men by this time it made some working days about 18 hours. It wasn't easy trying to set watches on such short passages. It was just as easy to stay on and give each other a spell at the wheel while the others were resting.

By 1970 the Lascar had gone and the Anzac[13] was full time on the 'Yanks' at the Holy Loch and the Glenshira[14] was ready for going. That left the Lady Isle, Lady Morven, Spartan and Kaffir as the last of the small puffers trading in the Clyde. The 'outside boats', as we called them, were the Glencloy, Glenfyne, Glenshiel, Glenshira, Dawnlight, Raylight and Stormlight.

The Stormlight had been converted from steam and had four Ford engines in her, the propeller shaft being belt driven using hydraulics. This was not a great success, as the belts quite often started slipping especially in bad weather when the propeller came out of the water. She was also pretty slow, doing only about

13 Built in the 1940s; traditional 66-ft long puffers.
14 Built in 1953, the first diesel puffer, 88ft long, 150 tons deadweight.

seven and a half knots. The *Moonlight* had been lost (see chapter 23) and the *Polarlight* and *Warlight* had gone. The puffer crews on the small boats being reduced to three men and the *Lady Morven* having a grab, self-discharges for the *Lady Isle* were a thing of the past. In a way this was a good thing as loading in Ayr late at night meant a very long day. Having to jump into the hold at the end of it and start shovelling wasn't much fun. We still traded out to Islay and met the usual gang.

Another run we still did in the summer was out to Tiree. This was my first run north of Islay as skipper and so was quite chuffed when everything went smoothly. We sailed from Ayr at two o'clock in the morning, which was about low water, was on the Mull for slack high water, caught the north-going tide and arrived in Tobermory at eight o'clock. We turned in for a few hours and sailed to catch high water at Scarinish. I felt pleased with myself when one of the lorry drivers came down and told me the coal merchant wasn't expecting us until the night's tide. The company had told him that, as there was only the three of us on board, we would probably stop over and sail through the day arriving on the night's tide.

The lorry driver got hold of the coal merchant and we started the discharge at ten o'clock. I telephoned the office and reported in that we were discharging and should finish by the next evening. They were surprised, but quite happy to hear this and told me I needed to wash the hold out as we were bound for Glenarm to load lime chippings, which were used in the building industry for rough casting. We finished as normal the next evening and sailed for Glenarm, washing the hold out on the way there.

The loading in Glenarm was the usual chute affair. Extra care had to be taken as the chippings would run badly to one side giving the boat a bad list. Quite often on completion of loading we had to wait until we floated to see if we had a list, which had to be trimmed by shovel before hatching up and sailing. On this occasion the chippings seemed to be carrying a lot of water which the engineer was continually pumping out on our passage to Ayr. Like all puffers and coasters, the *Lady Isle* had a water tight bulkhead between the hold and engine room with a hold bilge suction and change over valves for the engine room bilge system. Both worked off the same pump. Only, on the *Lady Isle* the hold bilge pipe had rotted away and couldn't be pumped in the normal safe manner. Rather than pay for a new pipe and valve which was seized solid, the owner had burned quite a large hole at the bottom of the bulkhead under the engine room plates so that any water in the hold ran through into the engine room and was pumped out that way.

The engineer seemed quite concerned by the amount of water in the hold. I went down to the engine room with him and had a look. The water was running steadily, was white in colour and looked as if it had come off the chippings. Plus, with our hosing down there was probably some water lying between the frames in the hold. I decided it was not a matter that would concern me further and we arrived safely in Ayr.

60

As we were discharging one or two of the ceiling boards were damaged by the shore crane and this required the local joiner to come and fix them. When the joiner appeared he lifted out a couple of boards and a jet of water shot into the air. The hold had been leaking after all. The normal practice was to pull a fish bolt with a rubber pad on it through the hole and bolt it up until a more permanent repair could be done in dry dock. To put a fish bolt in whilst the boat is floating requires a fair bit of skill and a good bit of luck.

What you do is this: you find a fish bolt about the same width as the hole or crack you are trying to plug and see if it fits. Sometimes any ragged edges have to be filed away. This is quite important. It is also a wet job. Most fish bolts have a tapered point with a hole through it. Take a ball of light, but strong line, tie a nail or something fairly heavy to it and feed it through the leak. Let out plenty of slack. Have two of the crew, one on either side, pull a heaving line along the keel catching the nail and light line and pull up to the surface. Attach the fish bolt to the light line and pull it through until the eye of the bolt appears through the leak. Gently work the bolt through the hole keeping the line attached. If the bolt jams, don't pull too hard, try and work the bolt free as the tighter the fit the stronger the job and you don't want to lose the bolt and have to start again. Once through and pulled tight the water should have eased off. Hold the bolt by the threads, take the line off, slip pad and washer and nut on and slip a nail through eye, then tighten bolt up. The leak should be stopped and the vessel safe.

On this occasion we pulled the fish bolt part way through when it jammed on a ragged edge and no amount of wriggling would free it. I was wet by this time. I took a hammer and tapped around the bolt, pulling quite hard on the line. The bolt came free okay but another two holes appeared about six inches apart, both letting in water. The joiner took one look and disappeared ashore mumbling about not working on a boat that was sinking.

'Huh! Landlubbers! They are ten a penny!'

We ended up putting three fish bolts in and then boxing this off and putting large cement box in. We put a few more cement boxes in her over the next two years. The joiner returned next day and finished the repair. We then loaded for Rothesay.

By the 1970's deep-sea ships were becoming fewer and fewer and a lot of deep-sea AB's[15] were moving to the North Sea and working in the oil and gas industry. Some came to the puffers; some men adapted to puffer life, some didn't. One deep-sea man who joined had been all round the world and would tell us he had been with Blue Star, Blue Funnel, P&O, Reardon Smith and the Red Cross shipping lines.

Anyway he couldn't box the compass or steer a puffer. We then gathered that puffermen were beneath him. On one particular day they had sailed from Ayr and

15 Able-bodied seamen.

were about two hours out heading for the Mull of Kintyre when the skipper came into the wheelhouse clutching a shoe lace. He placed one end of the lace on the chart at Ayr harbour and dropped the other end loosely in the direction they were heading. He then said to the AB, who was on the wheel, 'Do you see this end here, that's Ayr harbour breakwater where we have just come from. You see this end of the lace, that's where we are just now, okay?'

'Aye, what about it?' said the AB.

The skipper then put his finger on the end at Ayr harbour and stretched the lace in a straight line.

'Do you see where the end is now? That's where we bloody well should be if you tried steering in a straight line instead of bumming about how good you were deep sea. And another thing, you can't steer a compass course either. The mate had to tell you the course in degrees and nobody can steer a puffer by degrees, half points maybe.'

He was a quieter AB after that. It was hard to get good staff in those days.

CHAPTER 17

The Loss of the Kaffir

In September 1974 there was a very odd incident off Ayr. The *Kaffir* had loaded coal for Rothesay but was waiting on an engineer. Charlie Marr, the skipper, was near retirement age. He was very knowledgeable but very sentimental, especially if he had had a drink or two. An odd tear would come to his eye. John the deckhand had been a ship's cook deep sea and was actually quite young and intelligent and had all his chef's papers. He liked the puffers and was a real good shipmate. He had only one problem, he stuttered very badly and if excited found it really hard to get the words out.

Anyway, the *Kaffir* was loaded with coal and the skipper and deckhand were in the pub waiting on the engineer. Time went on. It was after eight o'clock and getting dark and no engineer had appeared. Just at that moment the off-duty pilot

MV *Kaffir* on the Clyde before her inglorious end off Ayr harbour in 1974. She was built in 1944 at Kirkintilloch as a VIC but the Admiralty cancelled the order. She was taken into Hay's fleet after World War II and converted to diesel propulsion in the 1962. *Courtesy of the Ballast Trust*

came into the pub for a drink before going home. He saw the skipper and deckhand sitting and wondered what was going on.

'Are you going on leave skipper and who's taken over from you?'

'No, we are waiting on an engineer arriving, he should have been here two hours ago,' moaned the skipper.

'Well, when I left the pilot house, the *Kaffir* had her navigation lights on and was manoeuvring in the dock and looked to be ready to leave.'

The puffers didn't have VHF radios in those days and provided there were no bigger ships sailing or arriving, could come and go quite freely from Ayr.

'Please, don't kid me on like that. I can't take it,' the skipper said as his laughter subsided.

'I'm not kidding skipper, the *Kaffir* is certainly moving in the dock.'

In a flash the deckhand left the pub and ran down to the pilot house just in time to see the *Kaffir's* stern light leaving the harbour. He ran to the pilot house and spoke to the duty pilot. By that time he was stuttering and stammering so much, the pilot thought he had missed his passage.

'Don't worry about it son, she's only going to Rothesay. You can stay here tonight and go to Rothesay in the morning.'

'B....b.....but the sk.....sk....skippers i.....in th...th...the p...p...pub!' he finally blurted out.

The pilot realised that something was wrong. Then the skipper and the off-duty pilot arrived. The skipper was in a sorry state.

'Someone has hijacked my boat, I'll kill them!' he bubbled.

All four stood and watched as the *Kaffir* zig-zagged about. One minute they could see the stern light, the next her starboard light then her masthead and sidelights.

'Aye, she's heading back in.'

'Oh no! She's not! The *Kaffir* doesn't know which way she is heading.'

The police and coastguard were telephoned. The pilot boat was launched. The pilot, police, skipper and deckhand went out to try and intercept the *Kaffir*. Unfortunately, they were too late. The *Kaffir* had left the harbour and run aground. The police arrested the only man on board ... the engineer. The skipper wanted to try and save the *Kaffir* but as it was a falling tide and a slight swell was running, the probability was that she was holed.

When questioned later about why he took the *Kaffir* away, the engineer's excuse was that when he arrived on board at six o'clock there was no-one there. So he made a cup of tea and waited for the crew to arrive. He then fell asleep in the mess room and when he woke up two hours later, thought the skipper and deckhand had turned in and to do them a favour, started the engine, let the ropes go and sailed, thinking the skipper would appear when he heard the noise of the engine. Once he cleared the harbour he had no idea in which direction to go and went to call the skipper. No skipper, no deckhand. Panic set in. He couldn't find the entrance; nothing but darkness in one direction and a mass of lights in the other. Totally confused he ran aground. The *Kaffir* was a total loss.

After the engineer was charged (technically with piracy), found guilty and let out after his jail sentence, he said, 'I was told I had to take the boat to Rothesay. If I had got the Kaffir to Rothesay that night there would not have been a word said. I would have been told not to do it again. The skipper would have got his wrist slapped for not being on board when I arrived. I telephoned the Ayr office and told the agent I would arrive at six o'clock. It's not my job to go looking round the pubs for the skipper.'

The view among the boys was that the engineer would be alright.

'Ach, he'll be alright, someone from the office will be waiting for him outside Barlinnie Prison when he is released. He'll be in line for promotion to skipper. He done the company a big favour, they'll get the insurance money.'

One skipper said that some skippers believed that the company had an agreement with the governor of Barlinnie Prison to let them know if there were any seamen inside looking for a job on their release. It wasn't true but was a standing joke when any dubious character appeared.

'Aye, he's jist oot o' the jile.' was the reply when someone asked who he was.

The next day the company had a good look round the *Kaffir* to see if it was possible to take the coal out and possibly salvage her. But as she had run aground on a falling tide she had holed herself and the next high water and swell had lifted her further onto the rocks making it unsafe to bring one of the bigger boats with their derricks alongside. The *Kaffir* was full of fuel, having taken on diesel prior to her demise. The company had an office and a well-equipped workshop right in front of where the *Kaffir* had grounded so our shore engineers decided they could possibly pump the diesel ashore before a pollution disaster occurred. After a lot of discussion on how to get the hose to the ship it was decided to use an old line-throwing appliance.

'Ah, but wait a minute, how far is it out to the Kaffir?' one engineer asked.

'Och, it is no more than two hundred metres,' someone else said.

'I think it is about three hundred metres, but what does it say on the apparatus?' the engineer super asked.

'Two hundred and seventy five metres. Aye, that'll be long enough. Look at the expiry date, do you think they will fire alright?'

'Oh, I don't know if we should use those, they look a bit dodgy.' the super said.

A bit more head scratching was going on amongst the engineers about what to do when the office manager appeared on the scene, a man who had never been to sea or seen an angry wave in his life.

'Has the *Kaffir* not got line-throwing apparatus on board? That will be in date, will it not?'

Problem solved. Everything was set up behind the workshop. Hose ready, pump ready. The two engineers rowed out to the *Kaffir*. The plan was to fire the line ashore, connect on the hose, start the *Kaffir's* winch and pull the hose out. Then set everything up and order a tanker for the next day to load the diesel and take it away. Pretty straightforward. The two engineers dug out the line-throwing apparatus and after reading the instructions five or six times decided they knew how it worked. Engineers being engineers they took off the front cover, took a turn with the looped end but didn't make it fast, signalled ashore that they were ready and fired. The rocket took off, the line shot out and carried on over the houses and up one of the streets, taking the line with it. The engineer super looked as if he was dancing to a Jimmy Shand record. The office manager was running after the trailing line trying to catch it. Whatever happened to the rocket and line was kept very quiet and why the police weren't involved is a mystery. It's maybe because nobody was injured.

The two engineers decided to take the rockets out and pull the line out by hand and row ashore with an end attached to the *Kaffir*. It turned out that the *Kaffir* was about four hundred metres from the shore so both lines were needed. The operation went smoothly after that although the engineer super was worried for a few days expecting the police to arrive asking for an explanation on how a ship's rescue rocket and two hundred metres plus of line had landed in the middle of Ayr. All part of puffer life.

What happened to the *Kaffir's* cargo of coal? Ask the good people of Ayr.

The wreck of the *Kaffir* lies off the entrance to Ayr harbour. Note that her wheelhouse is gone – 'salvaged', of course. From the presence of an inflatable dinghy tied to her stern we may presume that more salvage activity is underway?

CHAPTER 18

Characters

In the puffer days of the 60's and 70's there was a big turnaround of men coming and going and as no sea-going certificates were required at that time quite a few characters appeared.

The Lady Isle had one real worthy who came from Irvine; a good worker and a good laugh. He had been on the Lady Isle for about a month when we had to go to Troon for some reason; I think it was to have the shipyard do some welding and repairs. We arrived in Troon about eleven o'clock on Saturday night, too late for any buses. The Irvine deckhand decided he would get home somehow and started walking. I told him to be back at eight o'clock on Monday morning.

'Aye, no problem skipper, I'll be back then okay.'

And off he set. Monday morning arrived, no deckhand! Ten o'clock and still no sign of him. I was thinking that he had packed in, which was quite normal for deckhands. I nearly did it myself after the first fortnight on board. I had given him up when the police arrived.

'Have you a deckhand that works here?' the officer asked and mentioned the deckhand's name.

'Aye, but he has not turned up yet,' I replied.

'No, there isn't much chance of him turning up either. We just want to confirm he worked here, as he told us he was the deckhand on the Lady Isle.'

I was worried something had happened.

'Is he alright? Is he in hospital? What's happened?' I asked.

'He's in the jail. He stole a bus on Saturday night from the garage up the road here and drove it home. He parked it in the street where he lived, outside a neighbour's who saw him. Do you want him back?' the officer asked.

'Well, we are loading in Ayr this afternoon at four o'clock. Tell him to be there by then.'

He never turned up. What a character.

There was an engineer on the puffers who had been in the company a long time but had actually served his time as a baker before coming to sea. Charlie always got his priorities right. One night we were sitting in Greenock and Charlie got changed to go ashore. As I watched him walking up the quay wall he seemed to be limping rather badly and it looked as if he had injured his foot. I thought to myself that it was strange as he had never said anything about hurting his foot. I forgot all about the incident until about a week later when we were in Ayr. The mate came back from telephoning home and had passed Charlie on his way for a night ashore.

'I see old Charlie is limping badly, where did he hurt his foot?' the mate asked.

'Don't know, he was limping badly last weekend as well when we were in Greenock. He's never said anything about it. I'll ask him when I go ashore.'

I walked into the pub which wasn't very busy and there was Charlie pumping money into a one-armed bandit as if it was going out of fashion.

'For Christ's sake, stop throwing your money away on those machines, you'll never win. It's a mug's game,' I told him.

'That's about a tenner he's stuck in there. One of the dockers took twenty quid out of it at dinner time, so he's wasting his money,' the barmaid whispered to me.

'Hoi, by the way you old git, what have you done to your foot?'

'Nothing wrong with my foot, why?'

'Well, the mate saw you limping when you came ashore here and you were limping last week in Greenock. If you have injured your foot you should have said so. We would have got you to a hospital to have a look at it.'

'There's nothing wrong with my foot. I've no sole left on my shoe. I've got to walk on the side of my foot to stop the stones digging in and also keep my foot dry.'

This from a man who had just stuck a tenner in a one-armed bandit. He was a puffer engineer and a baker to trade. It makes you wonder!

'Charlie, you can buy a pair of Yankee shoes for ten bob. Go and see the boys on the garbage boat. They have dozens of pairs for sale.'

'Aye, I know. I bought this pair about two years ago and they are really comfortable. I hate parting with them.'

I gave up and ordered two whiskies.

Another interesting tale happened about the same time as the *Kaffir's* demise. The *Raylight* was in the side berth in Brodick discharging her cargo and being a little bit bigger stuck out slightly at the end of the pier. The ferry berthed okay on its first run with no problems but after arriving back in Ardrossan the wind started to pick up so the ferry captain telephoned the pier master at Brodick to ask if he could ask the *Raylight's* skipper to move off so he could come in at an angle and place the ferry's bow on the corner and put a spring on for safety's sake, and as the ferry was only in for a short time she could just lie off until she sailed. Of course, by the time the ferry captain had arranged all this the skipper, engineer and one of the deckhands were all in the Douglas Hotel, leaving the mate and the other deckhand discharging the cargo. The pier master waited until the ferry was about 15 minutes away before he told the crew to stop and clear off the berth. The mate shouted up that this couldn't be done as the skipper was not there. 'You'll need to go to the Douglas for the crew. I can't shift the boat on my own.'

The deckhand ran up to the Douglas and tried to get the skipper out and down on board. The engineer and deckhand left right away and by that time the ferry was standing off, waiting on the *Raylight* to leave. The skipper reluctantly left the bar after much coaxing by the pier master, who had arrived on the scene. He was in a foul mood and doing a lot of cursing and swearing. By the time he staggered down the pier, the ferry captain had lost patience and was just going alongside. The skipper was standing in the middle of the pier, fisherman's jersey up to his neck, hadn't shaved for about a week, grey hair standing up at the sides like horns. The ferry captain was on the wing of the bridge with the passengers all standing on the pier side of the ferry waiting to disembark.

'You are nothing but a Milanda bread carrier, a sea-going bus driver. Do you want me to fuckin' come up there and fuckin' show you how it is fuckin' done? You are fuckin' hopeless!' the skipper shouted drunkenly.

Some of the crew spotted the police coming down the pier and huckled the skipper on board before he was arrested. The ferry captain just shook his head. Some of the passengers were laughing at the antics of the skipper. We paid the price though because after that we had to shift out every time a ferry arrived, instead of just pulling back a bit. This really slowed the discharges down and gradually the two regular shovellers had to take other jobs as there were not enough puffers coming to Brodick to justify full-time work.

The skipper involved in the ferry incident told me another yarn in later years. Although it didn't involve a puffer, a pufferman was there. This young fisherman from the east coast, at the outbreak of war in 1939, had volunteered for the air force and joined bomber command where he remained until the end of the war. Not wanting to go back to the fishing, he managed to secure a job on a coaster where by 1960 he was a full-time captain in the company. The puffer skipper had left the puffers and was looking for a job. As luck would have it the coaster skipper needed a mate so our man got the job. The coaster was bound for Hamburg. They picked up the pilot at the mouth of the Elbe and as it was quite a long passage, the skipper and pilot were chatting away. Well, the pilot was doing most of the talking, the skipper just wanting to berth, clear customs, speak to the agent and turn in. It had been a hard passage across the North Sea.

'You haf been to Hamburg before captain? To my beautiful country ze Elbe is a wonderful river,' said the pilot, extolling the virtues of his country.

'Och, aye. I've been here hundreds o' times.'

'Ja! Zis is ferry strange. I haf been ze pilot on ze Elbe for many years and know most of my regular captains. I do not remember you.'

'Na, na! Ye widnae remember me,' the captain said. 'It wis during the war. I was at thirty thousand feet dropping bombs all over the place.'

The pilot went quiet, the captain yawned and went to fetch two bottles of beer and gave one to the pilot. There were no hard feelings.

I first met Crawford McDonald away back in 1966, about the same time I had met Terry Kelly. Crawford had trained as a psychiatric nurse and came to the puffers mainly during the summer months when he was on holiday and to relieve the mates or deckhands. He eventually went full-time. Crawford was always good for a laugh and full of practical jokes. One skipper remarked after meeting him once or twice, 'Are you sure he wasn't a mental patient, not a mental nurse?'

Though it was never proved who the practical joker was, Crawford and some of his crew got the blame. One deckhand who was built like a beanpole arrived in Ayr to be told there was mail for him. This was quite normal as Ayr was the main loading port and most letters were sent there and held until the puffer arrived. If it looked important, the letters would be sent onto the agents for delivery as soon as possible. This skinny deckhand collected his mail to find it was the first part of a Charles Atlas Body Building Course and could he send a cheque for such and such an amount and they would send on the second part of the course. The deckhand knew nothing about this as he certainly never ordered a bodybuilding course.

'I know I'm skinny, but I'm no a seven-stone weakling.'

Fourteen days later, he got a final demand. Either send the course back or pay up. He had no choice. He went to the post office and returned the course.

Another time one old engineer who was in his late 60's, but was quite a good-living chap and didn't go ashore much, received a sex aids catalogue. This didn't go down well and he threatened to go to the police.

'If these magazines get sent home, my wife will be highly embarrassed. There are no secrets in the village and the magazine is not even sent in a plain envelope. You can tell what it is by the cover.'

He was a very angry man for a while and quizzed a lot of people to find the culprit. One time I myself received some junk mail. This was from a dating agency. Send some money and all your personal details and we will send you six names of women who we think you will be compatible with. I knew it was a wind-up as I was not long married and had a good idea who it was.

It was all good fun and part of puffer life. Crawford left the puffers when the bigger boats appeared and ended up first mate on a survey vessel in the North Sea. He was a good shipmate.

CHAPTER 19

Spare Man

The *Lady Isle* was sold and I was now the spare man. For the next 18 months I moved about a lot, sailing with different skippers and sometimes relieving them for their holidays, gaining valuable experience on the way. I had now been over seven years at sea.

I sat on watch one night reminiscing about my days on the *Lady Isle* and *Lady Morven*, which had been partly owned by Captain McCorquodale and family, before the formation of Glenlight Shipping. I also gave some thought to my time helping out on farms prior to leaving school and there wasn't much difference between farmers and ship owners. Farmers were always on about the price of feed stuff for their cattle, the poor prices they received at the market for their calves or lambs, the cost of running a farm, etc.

Shipowners moaned about the poor freight rates, the cost of fuel, the cost of loading and the high wages they paid their skippers (!). In general both had a lot in common. I remember Captain McCorquodale saying to me one day, 'Keith, look after the pennies, the pounds will look after themselves.'

Very wise words which I sometimes wish I had listened to. I also remember other words of wisdom I was given by a farmer. I was helping out on a farm one day, during the school holidays. I was about 14 at the time. I just happened along one day as the farmer and his son were splitting a field in two and hoping I might get a shot at driving the tractor, started helping them out. As the fence was only temporary the posts were a good distance apart. The farmer was making the holes for the posts. I was holding the post steady until his son knocked them into the ground until they were firm. As the day wore on the farmer took his jacket off and as he walked past me put his hand on my shoulder in a friendly manner and said, 'Ye ken son, if ye hiv tae tak yer jaiket off tae make a pound, ye'll never be rich.' I just laughed, at that age not really understanding what he meant. If I had had a pound in 1958 I would have considered myself very rich indeed. Later on that day the farmer asked if I would come back for the rest of the week and help out. A couple of days later we were finishing off the fence, putting the barbed wire on. I was holding the wire against the post while the two of them stapled it. About mid-morning the farmer looked up and spotted someone coming across the field.

'Who's this coming? It'll be one of these bloody salesmen. They'll have the shirt off my back before they are finished,' the farmer cursed. This well-dressed gentleman approached; suit, shirt and tie and wearing wellington boots with the suit trousers tucked in.

'Good morning Mr Ferguson. How are you? It's a lovely day, is it not?' he said.

'It is my day off today and it being such a lovely day thought I would take a run out to the farm to see you.'

'Oh aye,' the farmer said suspiciously.

The farmer's son and myself both moved out of earshot. A couple of minutes later both returned to the farm. We carried on with the fence. The farmer returned about an hour later.

'See, whit did I tell ye? Whit did I tell ye the other day son? Never got his hands dirty, never took his jaiket off and yet he made money. I'm in the wrong job, I can tell you.'

'Who wis it faither?' the son asked.

'The bank manager. It's near the end o' the month and there were some bills to pay. He couldnae wait until I came into the bank to pay them, had to bring them to me. Aye! They never come out to offer you a loan when times are hard though. Ye've got to go in on bended knee and beg. I'm telling ye Keith, get a job in a bank or a lawyers office and keep your jaiket on. That way ye'll make money.' Forty-five years later I still laugh at that old farmer's words and I believe a lot of what he said is true.

I was on watch on the *Glenfyne*, which was a good boat to steer having a hydraulic helm which gave you time to check a chart or fill the log book in or reminisce. The skipper was elderly and had spent all his days on the puffers, about 45 years, and was widely experienced and knowledgeable. We had left Dalmuir Basin where we had loaded undersea telephone cables for three places, Ullapool, Oban and Iona. So we were for Ullapool first where we had to meet up with the crew of one of the GPO cable ships who were doing the cable laying along with the local engineers.

All went well. As I was supernumerary, we were working four on, eight off. The skipper came up every time during my night watch, which was midnight to four. I didn't think anything of this. We arrived in Ullapool, met up with the cable ship crew and two days later the job was completed. We were then on our way back to Oban for the next job which was to lay a cable across the Sound of Kerrera with the same crew and local GPO engineers. The skipper seemed a little on edge for some reason and came up twice during my watch.

'What's up skipper. Can't you sleep?' I asked pleasantly.

He checked the radar position, checked the chart, mumbled something and went back to his cabin. The mate came on at four and I said to him about the skipper being up twice during my watch.

'Oh, he'll be up during my watch as well. He's always the same. It's nerves. He lives on his nerves, as you'll find out the longer you are here,' the mate replied.

A grab full of sand is being unloaded at Loch Carnan on South Uist. The cargo derrick and the grab are being operated by the crewman in the 'box' next to the foot of the mast. Sand travelled both north and south in the puffer trade. This is commercial quarry sand going north but the puffer companies bought dredging rights from the Crown Estates and would use the grab to dredge sea sand from the beds of places like Onich Bank to take south after they had delivered a cargo to the islands. At one time a great deal of this sand was sold to Glasgow Corporation to put on the rails of the tramcars to prevent them skidding in icy weather. *Courtesy of the Ballast Trust*

I was 30 years old and couldn't understand how a skipper, who had spent 45 years at sea, could be bothered by nerves. He should have had the job down to a T. Thirty years later I know how he felt. As one old skipper said to me in a pub in Rothesay one night, with tears in his eyes, 'Aye, you will be an old man yourself someday, so don't laugh.'

'Huh! I'll never be like you lot,' I thought to myself.

Wrong! Old age and stress comes to us all. We completed the Oban job in the Sound of Kerrera and sailed out to Iona through the Torran Rocks. A nasty place in any swell and better done in daylight. The weather started to break, southerly wind and rain, the wind causing a nasty swell in the Sound of Iona where the cable was going across. We had to go round to Bunnessan for shelter where we lost two days. We were running low on stores, so I volunteered to walk the mile into the village and pick up what I could in the way of food. The skipper had gone ahead of me to telephone the office, so I met up with him on the way back. He told me I was supposed to transfer to the *Glencloy* but as we were held up by bad weather that had been cancelled. I mentioned that I was disappointed by this as I had never sailed on the *Glencloy* and wouldn't have minded doing so. Whether I offended him by saying this about the *Glencloy*, I don't know. A couple of minutes later he said to me, 'You know Keith, I don't think you have the potential to be a skipper on one of the bigger boats. It's okay sailing about the Clyde on the likes of the Spartan and Lady Isle but this is a different game. I think you need a lot more experience first.'

'Oh well, I seemed to manage to take the Spartan from Ardrossan to Stornoway last December. The company were happy enough and I think that is why I am with you on the Glenfyne, to take over one of these days. Did the company not tell you that?' I said smugly and walked on.

There was silence between us for the rest of the walk back. Later on the mate came to me and said, 'You have got him worried now. He thinks he is being sacked and you are going to be skipper. What did you say?'

'Oh, tell the old idiot not to be so stupid. I've got three years experience. He has been skipper for forty-five years. There is no way he will be sacked. And anyway, I don't want the job. He was being nasty so I was nasty back and he didn't like it.'

The weather eased off. The skipper seemed to cheer up. We laid the cable across the Sound of Iona. On completion we returned to Bunnessan and landed all the GPO gear ashore. As the *Glenfyne* was allowed 24 hours hire, on completion the skipper decided to stay and sail the next day as we were heading for Ayr and our cargo wasn't ready. We sailed in the morning and I stayed on with the skipper for the passage through the Torran Rocks so that I could gain experience and see how it was done. I officially came on at twelve o'clock. The skipper disappeared below. About an hour later he reappeared, checked the radar and went into the chart room and then came out wearing dark glasses. He said to me, 'Can you see Dubh Artach Lighthouse?' (This is a lighthouse that lies out to the west of Colonsay, is very tall and on a clear day can be seen for miles).

'Oh aye,' I replied. 'There it is on our starboard side, about twelve miles away.'

He took his dark glasses off and covered one eye with his hand.

'I can see it perfect with this eye.' He changed eyes.

'I can see it perfect with this eye as well.' He dropped his hand.

'I can see two lighthouses when I look normally.'

He shook his head and put his dark glasses on again. I didn't know what to say. He was the skipper. If it was an engineer, mate or a deckhand you would have told them to eff off and not be so bloody stupid. But not an old skipper with his experience.

'Skipper, when we go to Ayr have the company arrange for you to see an eye specialist and have you sight checked out. There is something wrong. If you like I will put a link call through for you and see if they can organise something for tomorrow.'

He agreed. I put a link call through. The company organised a specialist who checked him out and could find nothing wrong with his eyes. It must have been stress and nerves. It was the price you pay as you grow old.

I stayed on the *Glenfyne* for a few more weeks and then went to the *Raylight* to relieve the skipper there for his leave. The bigger boats were more comfortable to sail in, most having showers and washing machines; well, the *Glen* boats had. The company were pretty liberal when it came to paint and stores, so most skippers took pride in their vessels and, given the type of cargoes we carried, tried to keep their boats up to standard.

One skipper stood above us. His vessel was always smart. I'll not quote Para Handy here but his boat was the smartest. One Sunday afternoon the smartest boat was inbound for Rothesay. Once you were round Bogany Buoy you were quite close to the shore and as it was fairly deep you could follow the land round, just keeping a fair berth off until you reached the pier. The sun was shining, couples were out walking, kids were playing on the grass, elderly couples were sitting on the park benches. All were waving as the puffer passed. The skipper felt very proud. All these people waving at him, some of the kids pointing, a few whistling. Yes, it was good to be noticed. He felt very happy.

About 200 yards from the pier he slowed down and looked astern to check all was clear before he started manoeuvring. A sight then met his eyes. On the afterdeck and in full view the mate and the two deckhands were mooning at the people on the seafront. The skipper's face went from a healthy colour to red to purple in a few seconds but could do nothing about it as they were berthing in a couple of minutes. By the time they had tied up he had calmed down and saw the funny side of it.

The *Raylight* was a fine wee boat which carried about 180 tonnes and was very fast, doing about nine knots. She had been dogged by problems during her years, mainly engine and gearbox. The company had rectified this by putting a new engine and gearbox in, which helped for a while. She then had an engine breakdown in the Sound of Jura and drifted ashore. This was in late December 1972. The company salvaged her and she went back to sea again. It was after this that I joined her and would have liked to have stayed on as permanent skipper but it was not to be.

CHAPTER 20

Return Cargoes

I once again landed back out in Tiree on the *Raylight* with their coal cargo which wasn't a bad thing as I seemed to be the nominated skipper to go there regardless of what puffer I was on.

'Right Keith, you are loading for Tiree,' was the office's order.

I had been going there every summer since my first trip as deckhand on the *Lady Isle* and was on first name terms with a lot of the folk there. After Tiree the *Raylight* went out to Northbay on the Isle of Barra to load Barra shell for either Ayr or Glasgow.

How the shell evolved there I have no idea but there seemed to be thousands of tonnes of it. For loading onto the boats, it was washed and bagged and stored until a cargo was built up. The shell was used in the building industry. The shell cargo came up about every eight or nine weeks and was one of a few cargoes we picked up for the return to the Clyde. This was quite handy, especially in the winter when the weather was bad as it made the boat a bit more stable and she could handle a bit more weather when loaded.

Across from Barra on the Island of Skye there was a quarry a few miles south of Broadford at Torrin which produced high-quality white marble. A lot of this was crushed and used for rough-casting in the building industry. This was another good cargo for the puffers, as quite often we could be in the area with coal either in Portree or Broadford itself. It was just a matter of washing the hold out, making sure it was very clean and dry, having a night in port and loading next day. The marble was shipped as far south as Runcorn on the Manchester Ship Canal, so it was quite a long trip for a small vessel. These cargoes were usually done by the *Glencloy* and *Dawnlight* as they could carry about 240 tonnes and this made the trip more economical. They quite often managed to pick up a small cargo for the return to the Clyde. This was sometimes white salt for Carrickfergus, a small town in Belfast Lough. This was the cargo the *Moonlight* had when she was lost off the Isle of Man (see chapter 23).

The Skye marble was also shipped to Glasgow which was quite a good run as it was nice sailing up the Clyde in daylight, past all the shipyards which sadly were slowly dying out although one or two were still building fine ships. After Glasgow the boats usually went back to Ayr for coal or Greenock for the Holy Loch job with the Americans.

The other cargo we picked up in the Western Isles was dried seaweed. This was loaded in Lochboisdale, South Uist, Loch Maddy and Keos near Stornoway where Alginate Industries had factories. The seaweed was mainly harvested in the dozens of small lochs and inlets which dot the Outer Hebrides. It was also cut as far south as the west of Mull and in the Oban and Loch Sunart areas where it was then shipped by puffer to either Lochboisdale or Loch Maddy for drying and bagging before being shipped to Girvan where Alginate Industries had a processing plant.

The other cargo that was loaded was fishmeal in Stornoway. In the 70's, the herring fishing was still going strong so a lot of fishmeal was being made. This was mainly shipped to Southern Ireland, to Drogheda and Dublin. We usually came back to the Clyde 'lightship' after Ireland, which wasn't a good run especially if there was any easterly wind as, quite often, if there was too much swell, the pilot wouldn't take you in or out. Once the herring fishing stopped so did the fishmeal cargoes.

The same happened to the seaweed trade. Alginate Industries sold out to the management and workers who couldn't afford to build up a cargo and sent their product by road and ferry.[16] All this was happening by the late 70's and early 80's.

---

16 In actual fact Caledonian Macbrayne undercut the puffer freight rate by offering a very low rate for lorries to use their ferries. This caused a storm of protest about the highly subsidised public-owned ferry company attacking the private enterprise shipping companies.

CHAPTER 21

The Glencloy, Ghosts and Groundings

Raylight was bound for Ayr with a cargo of shell from Northbay on Barra. As there were no shops in Northbay and few in Tiree we were short of grub so decided to call in to Tobermory on our way south where we met the *Glencloy* and her motley crew. And of course we stopped for a while for a few beers in the Mishnish to find out the latest gossip.

The *Glencloy* had spent the weekend in Ayr. The skipper had gone home so the crew had had a wild time. The young mate loved his drink and partying but suffered terrible hangovers and had to have a drink to steady himself after a binge. So after having Saturday and Sunday in port he was in a terrible state by Monday morning. The skipper returned, the *Glencloy* loaded her cargo and prior to sailing they had a few beers. This made the mate feel worse.

When he came on watch at midnight he was really agitated, shaking and sweating and very jumpy. The second engineer brought him up a cup of tea halfway through the watch but he couldn't hold the cup, he was shaking so badly. The second engineer said he had a job to do in the engine room and went away with a wicked grin on his face. He went into his cabin and picked up a white sheet and then climbed through the escape hatch which led to the after-deck. He then crept along the deck to the side of the wheelhouse and waited until the moon had gone behind a cloud. He then tapped on the window and rose up with the white sheet covering his head and with his arms outstretched. The mate let out a scream and ran down to the cabins shouting out loud, 'I've seen a ghost, please help me! Oh, somebody help me! I can't go on!'

All three crew were in the messroom trying to pacify the mate. The skipper had given him a large whisky. The engineer had put the kettle on. The deckhand was trying to console him. The second engineer strolled into the mess room, wiping his hands on a rag.

'What's up with him?' he asked.

'I think you know something about this,' the skipper said.

'What's wrong? I've just come out of the engine room. I was fixing that water leak on the main geny.'

'Who's on the wheel then?' demanded the skipper.

'Probably the ghost that this nutter saw,' the chief replied, quite sarcastically.

With nobody in the wheelhouse the *Glencloy* was going round in circles. After the large whisky, which settled the mate a bit, the skipper told him to turn in and changed the watches. By the time they had reached Tobermory where we met them, everything was back to normal. The second had owned up to the prank. The mate swore revenge but nothing ever happened. They were soon the best of pals again.

On another occasion the *Glencloy* was on her way across the Minch. Same skipper, engineer; different mate and crew. The mate was on watch coming up for the Heisker.[17] This is a small island which lies to the west, off Canna and Rhum and has a lighthouse on it which was manned in those days. The mate fell asleep and the *Glencloy* ran ashore on the south-east corner of the Heisker in a small sandy cove. No damage was done that could be seen. No leaks in the hold or engine room. As it was nearing low water the skipper carefully assessed the situation and decided to leave things until the tide started flooding. Being the professional he was he had the crew launch the lifeboat and check round the stern for boulders and stones so as not to damage the propeller when going astern when she refloated. He also ran a kedge anchor out to pull her off.

The skipper and engineer both turned in leaving the mate, second engineer and deckhand to keep an eye on things when she started floating, hopefully three or four hours from then. Nobody had informed the Coast Guard. When daylight came the lighthouse keepers saw the *Glencloy* and came across to see if they could help. When they saw the situation and the crew explained they realised the vessel was in no danger. The tide was flooding by this time. Someone then mentioned they had never seen how a lighthouse worked and they were cordially invited ashore. All three jumped into the lifeboat and pulled themselves ashore, leaving the skipper and engineer asleep back on board.

Like most visits ashore, everything took time. They had to have a coffee, then a tour round the generator room before proceeding up to the lantern for a spectacular view across the Minch to the islands and to the mainland. The *Glencloy* was forgotten for a few moments. The skipper woke up suddenly thinking he had heard her bumping on the bottom. He looked out of the porthole. Yes, she was definitely moving. Where the hell was the crew? He should have been called. The engineer had heard the same and met the skipper in the alleyway.

'Where's the mate, the crew? You had better start up. They'll have bloody well have turned in. I think we are floating. I'll go and call them,' the skipper said.

By that time the *Glencloy* was starting to swing in towards the beach, only her bow was gripping. The skipper went up into the wheelhouse and found no crew. He went out on deck.

'Yoo, hoo! Skipper. Can you see us? We're up here! Yoo, hoo!' the crew shouted. They were at the top of the lighthouse. The skipper was dancing and tearing his hair out but could do nothing. The *Glencloy* was in danger of going

17 *Oigh Sgeir lighthouse.*

broadside to the beach and might have been stranded. The engine was started. The skipper had a quick look over the stern, which seemed clear enough, and decided to go for it leaving the crew to row out. All went well. The *Glencloy* came off without a scratch.

The crew rowed out and got a bollocking from the skipper. The passage carried on, the *Glencloy* had lost six hours; no damage to hull or propeller and he crew had a visit to a lighthouse. It was just another normal day for a pufferman.

MV *Glencloy*, (1966), on her trials, some years before her unplanned stay on 'Hyskeir'.

CHAPTER 22

Full-time Skipper of the Dawnlight

Would I go full-time skipper on the *Dawnlight*? I would! It was in the summer of 1974 and I had been eight years on the puffers. The *Dawnlight* carried a crew of five. A skipper, mate, engineer and two deckhands and had a working speed of nine knots. She was strongly built and when fully loaded and battened down was an able and very good sea boat in bad weather. I was to spend six happy years on her.

It was about that time that the company purchased the *Pibroch* from the whisky people[18] to replace the small boats, which had been reduced to two; the *Lady Morven* and the *Spartan*. The fleet by that time was down to *Glencloy*, *Glenfyne*, *Dawnlight*, *Raylight*, *Pibroch* and the two small boats plus the *Anzac* which was full-time on hire to the Americans in the Holy Loch.

The *Dawnlight* was completely different from the *Lady Isle*. The skipper, engineer and mate all had their own cabins, with the two deckhands sharing a large cabin. The skipper and engineers' cabin each had a washbasin with plenty of hot and cold water, with the mate and crew sharing a wash room and shower. The galley was well fitted out with a four-ring gas cooker, grill and oven, and a fridge with a decent-sized freezer box. The mess room could amply seat eight or nine people, which on occasion it did. The trading pattern of the *Dawnlight* was the same as the *Glencloy*, *Glenfyne*, etc: all of the West Coast of Scotland, Northern Ireland and east coast of Ireland as far south as Dublin, Isle of Man and North-west England. This was quite a large trading area for such small vessels especially in winter. It was happy work all the same as we made a lot of friends along the way.

Shortly after I joined, the *Dawnlight* went for her five-year survey which meant that her main engine and generators were stripped down and serviced. The engineer on board really knew his job, having served his time in the shipyards, so a top class job was done. On completion of her survey and repairs, which took about a month, she looked really smart: hull painted, name and load line marks all painted. We were again ready for sea.

Our first cargo was down to Ayr to load a cargo of coal for Port Ellen on Islay. The mate and one of the deckhands both came from Port Ellen, so managed a night at home. I hadn't been in Port Ellen for a very long time and was looking

18 *Scottish Malt Distillers of Elgin, a subsidiary of the Distillers Company Ltd.*

Built at Scott's of Greenock in 1965, for Ross & Marshall Ltd., MV *Dawnlight* was capable of carrying 240 tons of cargo. At 110-ft in length she was too big for the Crinan Canal but had the sea-keeping ability to go round the Mull of Kintyre with greater ease than the traditional 66-ft puffers. She was the author's first independent command.

forward to going back there.

'Who's skipper on here now?' I heard a voice say.

We were in Port Ellen and my cabin was next to the quay wall with the porthole open.

'It's Keith McGinn, do you know him?' the mate replied.

'McGinn, the bastard! Where is he? I haven't seen him for years.' I recognised the voice and went up on deck to be greeted by Philco and company.

'McGinn, it's good to see you. I remember when you were just a boy on the Lady Isle. The last time I saw you, you were in on the her in 1970. You had just finished a pipeline job at Irvine and this was your second or third cargo as skipper. Are you taking me for a dram?' he said, all in the one breath.

'Aye, Philco. That reminds me, have you got the two pounds you borrowed off me when I was a poor deckhand in 1966? I'll even tell you the date, it was the twenty-ninth of August and I had just been paid,' I jokingly said to him.

'Well McGinn, if you give me three pounds that'll be a fiver that I owe you and when you come ashore tonight you can buy a few more drinks.'

I just shook my head and went to the crane as the lorries had arrived. The *Dawnlight* was to call into Islay a lot during the next six years: Bruichladdich, Port Askaig, Bunnahabain Distillery and of course Port Ellen.

On the back wall of the Islay Hotel, Port Ellen there was a mural painted by a local artist Sean O'Leary. At least I think that was his last name. I knew him for about ten years and never really found exactly who he was or where he came from

He was a very educated man and spoke very clear Irish English, if you know what I mean! He always wore a kilt and had a very bushy beard and was a brilliant artist, as the mural in the Islay Hotel showed. When I was last in Islay in 2002, the hotel was starting to fall apart, as it had been closed for some time. It would be a shame if Sean's murals were lost. Sean had a little terrier called Mulldoon, a smart, cute little thing and when Sean came for a sail on the *Dawnlight*, Mulldoon came as well.

One particular time Sean and Mulldoon were over in Craighouse in Jura. Sean was doing a painting for the hotel so it was a case of free board and drink as payment for the mural. The *Stormlight* was on passage somewhere north to lay a cable for the GPO. As it was a terrible night with wind and rain, the skipper decided to try and make for Craighouse for shelter and wait out the storm. Coming through the entrance, nasty enough in good visibility, was pretty tough on the skipper in the strong wind and rain and when one of his four engines packed in, the wind took control and the *Stormlight* blew ashore and lay over on her side. The skipper managed to put a mayday call out and fired off a few rockets. The skipper and crew managed to huddle in the wheelhouse until the Islay lifeboat arrived and took them off. All four crew were okay but were very badly shaken by their ordeal, which happened so quickly. One minute they were coming through the entrance trying to pick up the beacon, get ropes ready, an engine went down and minutes later they were struggling for their lives. Very frightening.

Later on that night after all four were booked into the hotel where Sean and Mulldoon were staying. The crew were at the bar and were still badly shaken. Mulldoon was a friendly wee dog and didn't like to be ignored. He would come over to where you were standing or sitting and look up into your face and all you had to do was speak to him and give him a pet and away he would go, quite happy. If he thought you hadn't seen him, he would jump against your leg until you gave him a pet. The crew were standing at the bar talking about their bad experience, when Mulldoon strolled over and waited patiently to be noticed. This didn't happen. After going round all four crew to no avail he returned to the skipper. Still no response. Mulldoon then started growling and barking and grabbed the bottom of the skipper's trouser leg and started pulling like mad.

The skipper, who was still in shock from his shipwreck, thought he was being attacked by a mad dog, burst into tears and started shouting for help. Sean, who was at the other end of the bar shouted to Mulldoon, 'Leave the poor man alone, you don't know where he has been.'

Mulldoon let go and gave the skipper a dirty look. Sean, ever the opportunist, spoke up.

'And do you know my good friend McGinn. He was in Islay last week and bought me a few drinks. He speaks very highly of you and your crew skipper. Yes, I'll have a pint of Guinness and a whisky. Very kind of you. I'll tell McGinn I was speaking to you.'

I met the skipper about a month later and he told me about what happened and about Sean and Mulldoon. The *Stormlight* couldn't be saved. The crew were very lucky that she didn't roll over on impact losing all four lives.

There are a couple Sean's murals in the Jura Hotel and if you ever visit the place have a look at them. Sean and Mulldoon sailed on the *Dawnlight* a few times, going over to Portrush then Lochboisdale, Portree, Ardrossan, Mull, Red Bay, etc. One time he arrived in Ardrossan with one of the other puffers and decided to wash his socks on Sunday morning. Having just his kilt on and bare legs, he borrowed a coat and went for a walk along the dockside.

A woman in the flats opposite saw this bearded warrior, bare legs, wearing a coat, strolling up the quay, thought he was a flasher and called the police. By the time Sean reached the main street two patrol cars screeched to a halt beside him and ordered him to stop.

'Have you anything on under that coat, Sir?' one constable demanded.

'Oh, have a look officer and see what I've got.'

With this Sean whipped his coat open to reveal his kilt underneath. The police asked where he came from and what he was doing there, then went away quite happy when he told them he was off the puffer in the harbour.

I hadn't met Sean for a few months and when I did meet him there was no Mulldoon. So where was he?

'Well McGinn, it was like this, I was training him not to eat and just as I had him fully trained, the poor thing died on me and after all my hard work too.'

I didn't believe a word of this anyway and found out there had been an Irish yacht in Port Ellen and Mulldoon had gone back to Ireland on board and was happily in a good family home. Sean is no longer with us, having passed away a long time ago. He was a real life character all the same.

The *Dawnlight* had finished discharging and our orders were to load salt at Kilroot for Ullapool. That was the end of August 1974. We arrived in Ullapool at ten o'clock on the Friday and started discharging right away. Ullapool was very busy with holidaymakers from the large caravan park on the outskirts of the town. We didn't finish discharging on the Friday so went ashore at night where we saw a fellow busking on the street corner. He was a strange-looking chap, long hair, goatee beard, drainpipe trousers and winkle pickers and was playing a banjo. He came into the pub later on and I bought him a couple of drinks and found him really nice to talk to and he asked what we were doing there, so we told him. He played in the pub at night and with all the holidaymakers around it turned into a really good night.

We finished the cargo by dinnertime on Saturday and decided to stay overnight and sail on Sunday morning. The mate, two crew and myself ambled ashore and met Bill, our busker friend and a couple of Irish backpackers, who were hiking round Scotland. As it was half-past-two, closing time, we all chipped in for a carry out and went back on board the *Dawnlight* for a party. Our busker friend, Billy, saw us passing on the other side of the street and shouted across that he would be down later and to keep him a couple of cans. A few quiet drinks ended up a full-blown party, as more people saw us going on board and asked if they could join. Puffermen are party animals.

Billy, our busker friend, came on board. There were people in the galley, people in the mess room, people in the alleyway. Someone asked who I was. I told him. A fight broke out between one of the Irish boys and a local. I tried to stop it and ordered everybody off. Billy the busker just kept playing and drinking. Eventually calm returned. There were only the crew, Billy with his banjo and a couple of locals and the two Irish boys. The mate made a pile of sandwiches which were greatly appreciated by Billy and the Irish boys and a good time was had by all. Sunday morning arrived. We sailed back to Kilroot for salt. Billy went onto greater things and probably won't remember his time in Ullapool and being on board the *Dawnlight* one Saturday afternoon. I am still a fan to this day.

It was about a year later in August 1975, that the *Raylight* was lost. She was heading for Kilroot to load salt when she encountered a bank of fog just north of Larne. The watches had just been changed an hour before the fog came down, with the mate taking over. He hadn't checked what range the radar was set to and when he did look at the screen assumed that it was three miles with half-mile rings. In the dense fog he picked up a target which he thought was two miles away but was actually only one mile away, or six minutes sailing time instead of 12. It was not clear what the mate did next but a few minutes after checking the radar the *Raylight* ran onto the Maidens ripping her bottom out. The five crew managed to scramble into the life raft and were picked up by the Larne ferry that had seen the accident on radar. I liked the *Raylight* even though she had been dogged by bad luck, so was sorry to hear about her loss. At least no lives were lost.

Trade for the rest of the fleet carried on as normal. My pal Davie Langlands was skipper on the *Glenfyne*, Terry Kelly was skipper on the *Lady Morven*, the old skipper with the bad eyes was on the *Anzac* working with the Americans. He was quite happy with his little job and more relaxed.

I went on leave and attended the Nautical College to sit the Clyde Pilotage Licence. This allowed me to sail up and down the Clyde without a pilot. One old skipper who was due to sit the Pilotage exam arrived off Gourock and picked up the pilot and sailed to Glasgow. This was through the night. On the way up the river the skipper was telling the pilot he was sitting the exam in the morning and could the pilot give him any idea of the questions he might be asked. The pilot and skipper went through all the possible questions. The skipper did quite well and was reasonably confident. After berthing in Glasgow the skipper made his way to the Pilot Master's Office and was soon being examined. The Pilot Master asked a few questions which the skipper answered correctly. He was then asked

'What's the colour and number of flashes on Gourock Pier Head just outside the Pilot Station?'

'None,' the skipper replied.

'Oh yes, there is,' the Pilot Master said.

'Well, I picked up a pilot there at eleven o'clock last night and I never saw a flashing light.'

'Just a minute skipper,' the Pilot Master responded.

He picked up the telephone and phoned the Pilot Station at Gourock and asked them to check the light. They didn't know it was out and had been for at least 12 hours. The Pilot Master put the telephone down and turned to the skipper.

'Right skipper, I am not going to ask you any more questions. You have passed the exam. I have Pilots down at Gourock who are passing the light all the time and they didn't know it was out and you come in from sea and spot it right away. It shows you are very observant.'

It wasn't the answer he was supposed to give. He just happened to be off Gourock at the right time and gave what he saw or didn't see as his answer. Davie Langlands, Terry Kelly and I passed the pilotage exam, as did Tommy Ferguson, Davie Wilde and Jimmy Rory, over the next few years.

Salt north, seaweed south to Girvan, then up to Ayr for coal, were all part of *Dawnlight's* run for the next 12 months. The mate was on the *Lady Morven* with Terry. The Islay deckhand had packed in. Only the engineer remained as one of the original crew.

We carried on trading as normal, taking leave when we could be relieved. The engineer's wife wasn't feeling too well, so he asked for some extra time off and a new engineer joined. He had worked on fishing boats as engineman and seemed to know what he was talking about. But there was something strange about him. After the introductions were over and he had been shown round the engine room and was happy with everything I signed him on.

'Right skipper,' he said 'I hope there is no strong drink on this vessel. I don't touch the stuff myself now. I learned my lesson years ago. Strong drink and going to sea is a bad mixture. I hope your crew are a sober bunch. I won't tolerate drunkenness.'

'Wow!' I thought to myself, 'we've a real cracker here.'

'No, no, there is no drink allowed on board. When the work is finished and we are not sailing the crew can go ashore for a few beers but that is all. I run a tight ship,' I lied glibly.

Just as well he wasn't in Ullapool with us the summer before or Port Ellen for that matter. All went well. He was good with engines and always asked when we were sailing and had the engine started in plenty of time. But there was something not quite right and I couldn't put my finger on it. For the next fortnight we were kept very busy and didn't get much chance to go ashore as we were sailing or loading at the weekends. We arrived in Ayr one Tuesday to load coal on Wednesday for Lochmaddy in North Uist and I went home for a night as did the engineer. We loaded and sailed for Lochmaddy and arrived in the early hours of Friday morning. We were to load seaweed back for Girvan so would spend the weekend there. The mate said to me, 'I think the engineer is a secret drinker. He never looks drunk but always seems as if he has been drinking.'

'Well, he told me he hasn't taken a drink for years and he hasn't let us down in the engine room. But I agree, there is something not right about him.'

We finished the discharge in Lochmaddy on Saturday afternoon and wouldn't be loading until Monday so the rest of the weekend was free. The crew went ashore, as did the engineer who told me he was just going to the telephone and wouldn't be long, and sure enough I heard him going into his cabin about an hour later. As it had started to rain quite heavily I changed my mind and didn't go ashore and turned in about eleven o'clock. I heard the crew returning some time later.

Then it happened. About two o'clock in the morning my cabin door burst open and there was the engineer standing wide-eyed and gibbering,

'Skipper, come and put these women out of my cabin. I can't get to sleep for them. They won't leave me alone. You will have to do something about this. Naked women in my cabin!'

'Okay, okay, I'll come and put them out. Just go back to your cabin. You will be safe enough.'

I jumped out of my bunk and followed him to his cabin and thought about what to do next. It was all in his mind. He was hallucinating.

'There skipper. There is one standing there. Tell her to get out and get that one out of my bunk. I can't get to sleep for them.'

'Right girls, come on now, let the engineer go to sleep. You can come back and see him tomorrow. Go away home to your own beds,' I told the two imaginary girls.

'Thanks skipper, thanks very much. I can get to sleep now.'

I looked round the cabin which was strewn with empty special brew cans and an empty whisky bottle. What a mixture! No wonder he was in the state he was in. He was quite happy and went to sleep, so I closed his cabin door and turned in again. It was two in the morning.

About eight o'clock I had a cup of coffee and then made the Sunday breakfast and called the engineer and crew. I never mentioned a word about the women and when I looked in his cabin it was spotless. No empty tins or bottles. It was as if nothing had happened. But I know it did, because I hadn't been ashore on Saturday night. We loaded our cargo of seaweed for Girvan on Monday and as my regular engineer was due back, didn't feel it necessary to make a big deal about the engineer. But I promised myself that I wouldn't take him back again.

CHAPTER 23

Tragedies

During my time on the puffers there were quite a few good men lost one way or another. Some drownings were drink-related and some were accidents.

One particularly tragic loss was the young skipper of the *Raylight*, David McLeish, one night in port. He and the mate came back from a night ashore when they heard cries for help coming from the side of the ship. There was one of the deckhands stuck between the quay and the side of the ship, up to his waist in the water clinging to a fender but unable to pull himself out. He was starting to weaken with the cold when the skipper and the mate found him. The skipper lay over the bulwarks and got a rope under the deckhand's armpits and pulled it tight with the mate's help. They coaxed him to let go of the fender and move to a ladder about six feet along the quay.

The mate then went ashore with the end of the rope to try to pull the deckhand up the ladder. The deckhand was having difficulties climbing the ladder so the skipper leant over the bulwarks, grabbed his belt and tried to pull him up. The deckhand fell off he ladder and pulled the skipper in with him. The skipper was under the water and trapped by the fender.

The mate was frantic by then and started shouting to attract help. He srambled down the ladder and slapped the deckhand two or three times to try to revive him. The deckhand was smelling strongly of drink, but managed to get up the ladder. A couple of passers by came on the scene but the skipper had disappeared.

One of the men was a member of the lifeboat and ran to telephone for help, hoping the skipper had managed to swim out. It was not to be. They found the skippers body next morning, a tragic loss of a young skipper who was only trying to help one of his crew. The deckhand recovered okay and left the sea, never to return, at least not to the puffers.

One night 'The Monster' sailed from Liverpool bound for Carrickfergus with a cargo of salt. The forecast was southeasterly, force seven to nine, locally ten at times. Other coasters were going to anchor but 'The Monster' carried on. He decided to run before the weather and try and get round the Calf of Man before the worst of the storm broke. He would then have the shelter of the Isle of Man for the run up to Belfast Lough.

Just south of the Calf of Man the wind and sea picked up and then the cargo shifted causing the *Moonlight* to roll over. The skipper, engineer and two crewmen managed to scramble onto the hull in the horrendous conditions. A life raft floated free and one of the deckhands scrambled into it. He then managed to pull the other deckhand in and was trying to get John and the engineer in as well when a lump of water washed both men off the hull. They were never seen again. The Isle of Man lifeboat rescued the two deckhands sometime later.

Nobody could understand why 'The Monster' went on the course he did. Other puffer skippers reckoned that with a south-easterly wind, he should have run up the land past Barrow in Furness towards St Bees Head and then run for the Mull of Galloway. He would have been in reasonably sheltered waters. But that's the way it goes. One old skipper remarked when told the sad news, 'Well, he has been asking for it for years. That's why he was called "The Monster".'

In 1976 the old skipper, who had been on the *Glenfyne* for years, Johnnie McGuire was drowned in the Holy Loch whilst working for the Americans. It seems he had gone on board the dry-dock to tell them he had a lift for them. He was a long time coming back so the crew went to look for him. They spoke to the officer in charge, who informed them he had spoken to Johnnie ten minutes previously and was organising a crew to take the lift off the puffer. The crew returned on board and checked the hold and his cabin. Johnnie couldn't be found. The alarm was raised and very sadly the old skipper was found floating beside one of the dry-dock anchor chains, a tragic accident to happen to a man who had spent a lifetime at sea, sailing on the puffers in the days of steam, right through to the modern diesel vessels. He was back to one of the small ones to spend the time until his retirement, a handy little job to finish off a career that spanned over 45 years.

CHAPTER 24

Changing Times

By the summer of 1975 word was going round that the company was after a fleet of small coasters to replace the puffers that had been lost or scrapped and there was word of a concrete oil platform being built at Kishorn. Who was going as skipper and who wanted one of the new boats? The rumours were rife. I had already made up my mind that I would stay on the *Dawnlight* as the bigger boats didn't appeal to me and the accommodation wasn't as good.

The new coasters arrived.[19] I was asked if I would take one, but decided to stay on the *Dawnlight* meantime. Davie took one and two or three of the coasters' delivery crews and skipper stayed with the company and, of course, the new nicknames arrived as well. Davie Langlands was still 'Big Davie', Terry Kelly was still 'Kelly', there was 'Pilot Hamburg' and 'Brodick Ferry', 'Big Tam', an ex-trawler skipper and 'Old Bert' an ex-trawler engineer who was soon to become my regular engineer on the *Dawnlight*. Oh, and there was 'God', a skipper who thought he knew everything.

With characters like Crawford Kelly, the Bell Ringer, Old Faither, etc, we were a fairly close-knit community and stuck together.

I was on the phone to the office for orders. 'Okay, if you don't finish give us a ring in the morning and if you do finish head south, call in someplace and telephone. We have a couple of cargoes of coal to shift and are waiting to hear from the coal board as to the availability of coal. We will know by tomorrow morning.'

As it happened the lorries returned and we finished early and headed south. By 8.30 we had rounded Ardnamurchan Point and were into the Sound of Mull. As it was still only March the weather wasn't very good. We had a strong east-southeast wind blowing and it was very gusty so I headed for Tobermory.

It was not very nice at Tobermory Pier as the wind and swell were blowing straight onto the pier. If there was any east or south-east wind, damage could have been done to the boat and the pier. I didn't have many options as we had to have some grub as well, in case we couldn't get round the Mull of Kintyre, if the

---

19 *A fleet of five 400-tonne deadweight coasters were acquired to supplement the older fleet. One of these could carry half as much cargo again as the Glencloy and Dawnlight. They were re-named Raylight, Polarlight, Glenetive, Glenrosa and Sealight. Glenlight had a contract to supply thousands of tons of stone from a quarry at Kyleakin to the Howard Doris oil platform construction site at Loch Kishorn.*

easterly wind continued. We went into the bay and looked at the pier, which was empty. Conditions were not good. The sea was quite rough. I said to the mate and deckhand, 'If I stick the Dawnlight's bow alongside, do you think you can jump ashore, phone and get some grub? I will pull off and come back in and pick the both of you up.'

Both were quite happy to do this as both were young men and pretty fit. I stuck the bow alongside and hit the pier very hard. They both jumped ashore and I hauled off. Twenty minutes later I did the same again and both jumped back on board. I then backed off the pier and headed back into the Sound and headed south.

Our orders were to head for Ayr and load coal for Tobermory. During the day and evening the wind died away and two days later we were back in Tobermory. I checked the pier where I hit, there didn't seem to be any damage and the pier master had not complained and the *Dawnlight* hadn't been damaged. Everything was okay. That night we went ashore to the Mishnish and were standing at the bar when one of the local worthies said, 'Oh, hello Captain. That's a fine ship you have there. A fine wee vessel and you can fairly handle her Captain. Your crew are very fit, a fine bunch of men. I was watching you coming alongside the other day in that breeze of wind. You hardly touched the pier. Your crew were only seconds and they were ashore. What a fine piece of seamanship. Yes! A fine piece of seamanship and she's well painted too.'

All this said in a soft highland lilt. Inwardly I was laughing as I looked at his empty whisky glass and pint glass with about an inch of beer in it. Willie the barman kept looking across. 'Keith,' I said to myself, 'you are about to be tapped here, beat him to it.'

'Can I buy you a drink, sir?'

'Oh no, Captain. Not at all. I was just thinking that maybe you had a wee drop of paint I could have. I have a small dinghy that I am painting just now ready for the summer and I am a bit short of paint.'

'What colour had you in mind?' I asked.

'Oh any colour, Captain, any colour. And do you have a brush I could have as well and did you mention you would buy me a drink? You are a real gentleman Captain, a real gentleman.'

I must have been the softest touch on the puffers. I didn't get the chance to buy the local worthy a drink. Willie the barman came across.

'Right you, out. There's nobody tapping drink in this bar. Now out you go. You have been in here all afternoon and you have only bought about three drinks. Leave the customers alone.'

The worthy shuffled out the door. Willie then turned to me.

'Keith, don't give him any paint unless the tin has been opened. If you give him a full one he will only sell it and the same with paint brushes. Never give him a new one. Kai was in here last week and gave him a tin of golden brown and a brush. He does the same with all the puffer men and trawlermen that come in here. If you don't know him he butters you up and then taps you for something. A packet of soap powder, a fry of fish, a lump of rope or paint. Don't do it.'

The next day unbeknown to Willie, I gave the old guy a tin of paint and a brush. I just couldn't say no. The old worthy didn't have much.

The mate on the *Dawnlight* was a Campbeltown man who went by the nickname of 'King of the Road'. Alick had been on and off the puffers for years. Regardless of where he was, night or day, if he got fed up being at sea, he would up sticks and go and start walking until he got a lift or reached a bus stop. One skipper reckoned Alick would take a lift even if it was going in the wrong direction from where he wanted to go. Hence the name, 'King of the Road'. Alick stayed on the *Dawnlight* for over a year and then left, as was expected. He was a good mate and knew his job.

By 1976 Kishorn had started up so all the 400-ton-coaster-size vessels were employed up at Kyle/Kishorn, etc. This left the *Dawnlight*, *Glenfyne*, *Glencloy*, *Pibroch* and *Lady Morven* for the West Highlands. A new mate had joined the *Dawnlight*, an Ayr man by the name of Mick Murphy. Mick had just spent a month on the *Glencloy*. 'King of the Road' had gone. Another year had passed and Kishorn was in full production. My regular engineer was part of the shore team and was based at Kishorn to keep the coaster fleet going. As the boats were running 24 hours per day, every day, an engineer had to be on standby all the time. They did a week on, week off. Bert, the trawler engineer was then my regular chief.

Mick had long hair and looked about 30 years of age, but was actually 48. He told me he fished out of Grimbsy for 20 years, was in the army for ten, owned his own fishing boat and drove long distance for years. Bert shook his head and walked away when he told us all this.

We passed Tobermory on our way south and spotted the *Glenfyne* lying at the pier along with the *Lady Morven* and as we were not loading until Monday decided to spend Saturday night there and have a crack with Kelly and the gang. The engineer on the *Lady Morven* was an ex-army man, so we passed this onto Mick. Kelly, John, the skipper of the *Lady Morven*, who was my original mate on the *Dawnlight* and myself were sitting in the bar in the Mishnish. Mick and the ex-army man were sitting together at the bar. We all heard Mick say, 'So you were in Aden during the crisis there. So was I. We were parachuted in, scary stuff.'

Kelly tapped me with his foot and nodded towards the bar. The conversation carried on with Mick doing most of the talking.

'I was only in Aden for 48 hours, when I was called in front of the CO. "Murphy!" he said to me. "I see by your records that you are an ex-trawlerman, a professional seaman. I think you are more needed back on board the aircraft carrier. They need someone with your qualifications to help them run that ship. So off you go. We will try and manage without you." I can tell you mister, that's the truth. I kid you not.'

Well, Kelly, John and myself burst out laughing and nearly fell off our chairs. I made an excuse and went to the toilet to dry my eyes. I had heard some cracking stories in my time, but this was the best. The ex-army man followed me into the toilet.

'That man is the biggest fuckin' liar I have ever met. Is he mate with you? Pity help you.'

'I am afraid so,' I replied.

But it was all good fun.

I decided the next morning, it might be better to leave Tobermory, if only for the mate's health. There was no malice in Mick, he would actually go out of his way to help you. But, boy! Could he tell a story!

We had just finished discharging cargo in Oban and I had picked up the papers prior to sailing. It was flat calm, good visibility, a really nice day. Mick was on the wheel and I was reading a piece about a coaster that had been in trouble in the Pentland Firth but had been rescued before being driven aground in the horrendous tides and swell that can get up in that area. I had never been there but knew it was a dangerous place in bad weather. Bert said, 'It's a horrible place. You don't want to go there, Keith, unless you have to.'

Mick chipped in, 'Don't be kidded, mister, I'm telling you it's terrible. I was on a GY trawler once coming through there and a lump of water hit us. The wheelhouse got pushed back four inches! I got thrown into the corner and hurt my back. You know what the skipper said? "Murphy! Don't you lie there in the corner. Get back on the wheel right now and keep her steady".'

Bert made his excuses and went below. I tried not to laugh. I looked across at Mick. He was gripping the wheel tightly and staring straight ahead. A trickle of saliva was running down his chin. I thought, 'My God! He's not on the Dawnlight. He is on an imaginary trawler battling to save the vessel in the Pentland Firth!'

'Mick! Mick!' I shouted, 'are you all right?'

He looked blankly at me. 'Aye, aye, I'm all right. What's wrong?'

'Oh nothing, I just wondered if you wanted a read at the papers.'

Though we met the odd character in our travels, a lot of serious work went on most of the time. Cargoes loaded, cargoes delivered. Back to sea, load again and so on. The *Dawnlight*, *Glenfyne*, *Glencloy* were carrying about 90 cargoes each every year and doing the American hire for three to four days each month. So it wasn't all pubs and laughs. We were all working on average about 84 hours per week and grabbed a night ashore when we could.

Kelly was our gang leader and was good company. He was well-liked wherever he went and knew the best pubs in which to get a sub or a lock-in and where all the women hung out. Many years later, after first meeting Kelly, we were standing in a pub having a drink when the owner said to me, 'Where's Kelly? We haven't seen him for weeks. What a crew they are.' I told him where I thought they were.

'Kelly and his crew came in here about a month ago. Skint, needed money for food and cigarettes. The money I gave them they spent behind the bar and still went away skint. They asked my wife for a loaf to see them through till payday. I haven't seen them since. What a crowd!' he said laughing and shaking his head.

'I take it he owes you money. Don't worry, Kelly will be back in someday. He's honest that way.'

'No, no,' the owner said. 'The funny thing is a registered envelope arrived last week with the money and a note apologising for the delay. Aye, you puffermen are alright.'

Good old Kelly!

Another time we were in the Ship Inn at Ayr where the landlord had a notice above the bar that read:

'I had a friend, I loaned him ten,
I never saw the swine again!
NO SUBS'

Kelly challenged the landlord, 'What do you mean 'no subs' boss? We always pay you back.'

'Aye well, Kelly, it's just like this. One of your shipmates, Big Hughie Sorrel borrowed ten pounds off me two weeks ago and never paid it back. I just heard this morning he's done a runner, the bastard.'

Kelly replied, 'But, boss he wisnae one of my crew, or Big McGinn's. He's nothing to do with us.'

'He was a pufferman, one of you lot, and that's good enough for me. You will have to pay me back the tenner. It's your responsibility.'

'We're not paying! No way!' four or five of us said in unison.

'Aye, you'll pay it back with interest because every time you order a round I'll add five or six pence to it. You never check your change anyway. If you want drink somewhere else, go ahead. I know you will be back because this is where the women hang out. So I'll get my money back. Nobody does me out of a tenner.'

Big Hughie was never seen again. We would have been cheaper clubbing together and paying the money back there and then!

The *Glenfyne* had called in to Tobermory pier. Kelly and his crew were waiting to sail out to Tiree to catch the six o'clock high water at Scarinish. This was quite normal practice if there was a swell running at Tiree, as there were not many places to anchor and trying to lie at Gott Bay pier was no good because of the run and broken ropes the boat suffered. The *Glenfyne* arrived at Scarinish on the tide. The discharge went on okay. The tubs had been done away with. The coal was being measured by grab and unloaded by the crew. Cash in the hand. In the morning after the *Glenfyne* had sailed from Tobermory, a local woman reported to the police that her prize pedigree cat had disappeared the previous evening.

'Okay, Mrs Smith, can you give me a full description of the cat and where it was last seen?' asked the sergeant.

'Yes, Fluffy was last seen at the main pier about eleven o'clock. There was a puffer lying alongside at that time. The Glen something. I couldn't make out its full name. I hope the crew haven't stolen Fluffy. She's worth a lot of money.'

'Okay, Mrs Smith. We'll look into it. Don't worry, Fluffy will probably turn up. Cats like to wander.'

The enquiries were left at that meantime. In those days the ferry to Coll and Tiree called into Tobermory on her way out to pick up any freight or passengers for the islands. In this instance the local police sergeant had some business on Tiree and came out on the ferry. On finishing his business the sergeant and local constable were passing Scarinish when they spotted the puffer which had finished discharging and was waiting for the tide. The crew were in the pub spending their discharge money.

'I wonder if that was the puffer that was in Tobermory the other night when the cat went missing. We better go and check it out just in case it jumped on board and is hiding somewhere,' said the sergeant.

As the police car had to pass the pub on its way to the pier, Kelly and his crew saw the sergeant and constable going on board. Kelly, being the alarmist he was wondered out loud, 'What have I done. No! I don't think I've done anything wrong. I wonder what they want. It can't be me they are looking for.'

With that he rushed down the pier and jumped on board. The sergeant was having a look in the cabins. The constable was in the galley.

'What's wrong, what have I done? What do you want? I'm the skipper,' screamed Kelly.

'Were you in Tobermory the other night skipper and sailed about two o'clock in the morning?' asked the stern-faced sergeant.

'Aye, aye. That was us. But we didn't do anything, honest.' Kelly in a flap.

'There is a prize cat missing from Tobermory and it was last seen on the pier when you were alongside. We have reason to believe it may be on board here.'

'Sergeant, what's this cooking in this pot, it smells good.' As the constable lifted the lid from a pot that was simmering on the stove.

'That's stew, honest. Oh, please we wouldn't eat the cat. Ask the crew. We never saw the cat, honest.'

'Well, if you do find it on board, it's name is Fluffy and belongs to Mrs Smith. She will probably give you a reward for it's safe return.'

With that the constable and sergeant departed. Both smiling gleefully. By the time the sergeant arrived back in Tobermory, Fluffy had turned up and a few months later Mrs Smith had a few extra mouths to feed, though not pedigree ones.

CHAPTER 25

A Rescue (1)

One Sunday morning in 1978 the *Glenfyne* was coming round the Mull of Kintyre bound for Ayr when the crew spotted somebody waving wildly from a dinghy close into the rocks. It turned out to be one of the lighthouse keepers out checking a few lobster pots when his outboard motor had packed in. Though not in any immediate danger, he reckoned he would have managed to row back round the Mull to the landing place below the light. If you are sailing round the Mull someday go in close to the rocks. Just below the light there you will see steps and a small harbour where a dinghy can land.

The lighthouse keeper and Kelly, for he was the skipper, decided it would be safer to proceed to Campbeltown where the dinghy could be picked up. Kelly put a link call through to the lighthouse keeper's wife explaining what had happened and ask her to come over to Campbeltown and pick up her husband and dinghy.

'You're Kelly,' said the lighthouse keeper, 'I've heard a lot about you. Pleased to meet you.'

As they introduced themselves Kelly was presented with the biggest of the lobsters the lighthouse keeper had caught. To a pufferman this was the highest of honours, the crème de la crème, a real honour indeed. On arrival in Campbeltown the lighthouse keeper asked Kelly if he would wait and lift the dinghy onto the trailer when his wife arrived. It was decided the lobster would be Sunday night's dinner, along with all the trimmings. As Kelly hadn't tasted lobster before, this was to be a real feast, a party. They got a sub from a friendly barman, bought some beer and enjoyed themselves. I think they had forgotten they were bound for Ayr. What actually happened was that the lighthouse keeper sold his lobsters to one of the hotels and returned to the *Glenfyne* with a large carryout; whisky, beer, etc. The lobster by this time had been cooked and was cooling in the pot.

'Here you are boys. Thanks for saving my life. We'll have a couple of drams until my wife arrives, then I'll need to go.'

The partying started early and by opening time at 12.30, the lighthouse keeper had gone, the lobster was still cooling and all the trimmings had been purchased. A feast awaited.

'Hey, boys, it's half past twelve. The pubs are open. We will go up and get a sub, have a few pints and drink the rest of the carry out when we come back.'

'I'm not going to the pub, I've had enough,' the engineer said.

'Don't you touch that lobster. I'll fucking kill you if you do and don't drink all the drink you greedy bastard,' Kelly warned him.

The engineer was known to help himself to an extra sausage or a rasher or two of bacon when nobody was watching. Kelly and the remaining crew adjourned to the pub where they got their sub and were in full party mood with a few of the locals.

'Where are you bound today Kelly?' asked the barman.

'Oh, bloody hell! We're bound for Ayr. We are not supposed to be in here. I told the missus I would be in Ayr about twelve o'clock. What time is it now?'

'Half past three.' Kelly calmed down.

'Oh well. We were on a rescue mission. We will just finish our drink and get going. When we go on board, we'll start up, let the ropes go and sail. We can have our dinner on the way across.'

A shock awaited them when they staggered on board. The engineer was lying in the messroom in a drunken sleep, most of the carry out had gone and the messroom table was covered with bits of empty lobster claws and shell. The engineer had bits of lobster sticking to his shirt and trousers. What a mess! Kelly had turned purple. He slapped and kicked the engineer.

You dirty, greedy bastard! None of us has tasted lobster and you go and eat the lot.'

'I never touched the lobster,' the engineer drunkenly slurred as he tried to get up but stood on a piece of shell which pierced his foot.

He then collapsed in a heap on the floor where Kelly left him. Terry never tasted his lobster but got a roasting from his wife when he arrived in Ayr nine hours late. His wife had been waiting for him all that time in the Harbour Bar.

CHAPTER 26

Deck Cargo

When the puffers were in some of the island ports we were sometimes asked to take a deck cargo for one of the locals, if we were going to the same place as the cargo. This could be a small horsebox or a small boat. Sometimes even an old tractor. The person concerned would telephone the company and ask for a price. The company would quite often just say, 'Oh, see the skipper and if he wants to take it we don't mind. The puffer is going there anyway.'

This kept good relations between the islanders and the puffers. We often left it to the person to make up his mind what it was worth and pay us accordingly, all straightforward stuff. Sling the goods, lift it on board with the crane or derrick, lash it down and we were on our way. At the arrival port, same thing. Lift the goods ashore, no problems. But not all the time.

The *Dawnlight* was in Red Bay, Northern Ireland this particular Saturday, loading a cargo of agricultural lime for the farms on Islay, to discharge at Port Ellen. Lime is and was one of the dirtiest cargoes the puffers loaded, as the lime dust got everywhere, and I mean everywhere! All portholes had to be battened down, doors and ventilators closed and it still got into the accommodation. It stuck to the decks, rails, wheelhouse windows, clothes, hair, etc. The weather this Saturday was fair with just a light breeze so the dust wasn't too bad. Just a light covering everywhere. Loading was going well and by three o'clock we had about 40 tons to go and were awaiting the return of the lorries when a cattle float appeared on the pier. Out jumped an elderly gentleman and a young fellow.

'How are yous doing, boys? I'm looking for Keith, Keith McGinns' the man that'll do the job for me,' so said the Irish lorry driver.

'Er, I'm Keith McGinn,' I said cautiously.

'I was speaking to your Mr Pollock in the Glasgow office the other day and he said, see Keith when he is in Red Bay loading on Saturday and if any person can help you out he will. Ah, be Jezus, he's a nice fella that Mr Pollock, a nice fella!'

'Well, if I can, I will. What is it you want done?'

I was thinking it might be a piece of farm equipment that he wanted taken to Islay.

'Me daughter got married to a farmer on Islay and lives over there now and I have this piece of furniture to get over to her. It's a wedding present from me mother to her granddaughter and has been in the family for years.'

'A piece of furniture! Do you see the mess the boat's in with lime? It'll be ruined by the time we get to Islay. No way. Take it by ferry,' I replied.

'Oh, be Jezus, Keith. Do you know how much it would cost to go to Islay from here? A ferry from Larne to Stranraer. Then the long drive to Glasgow, then up to Loch Lomondside and on down to Kennacraig and a ferry to Islay and then all the way back. We just can't afford it. You are our only hope. So please say you'll do it. It means such a lot to me mother.'

'Well, it might get covered in lime but we will do our best to cover it and keep it clean. What is it anyway?' I asked.

'It's a grand piano', he said.

'Oh, for fucksake. How are we supposed to handle this?' I shouted out. The crew shook their heads in disbelief. The engineer came out of the accommodation and when I told him what we were taking to Islay shook his head and didn't want to know. I thought to myself, 'Pollock, you bastard. why didn't you ask what it was and tell this guy it was lime we were loading and no way could we take it, instead of putting the onus on the skipper?'

'Me mother was a music teacher and also a concert pianist and me mother would like her granddaughter to have the piano. It would make the old lady very proud knowing the piano was being kept in the family.'

Oh, for God's sake, stop, I thought, as I wiped away a tear. (It was just a piece of lime in my eye.)

'Okay, we will take the piano for you but I will not be held responsible for any lime that gets into the works, as you can see the state of the boat.'

'Don't worry about that Keith. We have a couple of old sheets to cover the piano with once we get it on board,' he said and then reversed the lorry and lowered the tailgate. This beautiful piece of work was sitting in amongst straw and cow dung. The piano must have been worth thousands of pounds but he didn't seem concerned. I never realised how heavy one of those pianos was but with the four of us and himself and his son we got it onto the quay wall.

'We will just drive the lorry up the pier in case we block the lime lorries when they arrive and then come back and help you lift it on board, okay?'

The two of them jumped into the lorry and drove off. They didn't stop further up the pier, but carried on up past Waterfoot village and out into the country. We were left with the piano whether we wanted it or not. The dirty swines. I didn't even have a telephone number for them. He had told me his daughter would be down when we arrived in Islay and would see us alright, cash wise. So at least we would get something out of it. After much groaning and grunting and with the help of the two loaders the grand piano was on board with very little damage. Just a couple of scrapes and one leg slightly loose. Luckily the *Dawnlight* had fairly wide decks at the stern of the wheelhouse and by shifting a 45-gallon drum of oil, the piano fitted in. We covered it as best we could with the two sheets and hoped it wouldn't rain or that salt spray got into it. It was such a fine piece of work, some German make, which we should never have been asked to take. All the crew agreed.

The two lorries of lime arrived and started loading, which was done by conveyor belt. Luckily the light wind had changed direction and the dust blew the other way over the bow. Loading completed, the crew hatched up and we set sail for Port Ellen arriving late on Saturday night. We were not discharging until Monday so had Sunday off, provided we got rid of the piano. The usual gang appeared; Philco, Nazzer, wee Bruce, Sean and the usual comments.

'Give us a tune, McGinn. How about a Russ Conway number or something classical. Got your own orchestra with you now.'

'Go away you bloody pests. You have no idea the worry this has caused me. I just hope no lime got into the works.' I replied.

Soon after a float appeared and a man and woman jumped out to collect the piano. She started moaning to me about the couple of scrapes and the little amount of lime that was sticking to the legs. What did she want? She got her piano over for little or nothing and I told her so. I didn't know whether the company were going to send her a bill if I did the job, so only asked for the price of a couple of rounds of drink for the crew. After much moaning on the woman's part the piano was loaded into the cattle float, which was much cleaner than the one that it had arrived in. Never again would I be talked into taking something like that again, I said to the crew after the lorry disappeared through the village. By 12.30 we were all in the pub. The piano forgotten about.

On Monday I telephoned the office and told Mr Pollock that the piano was delivered with a minimum of damage but for goodness sake don't ask us to do something like this again.

'What piano? I know nothing about a grand piano. The manager of the Glenarim Quarry mentioned a while ago that he had a farmer friend who had some furniture to go to Islay first time one of the boats was going there and could he stick it on the boat if the skipper agreed. We didn't want involved as it usually costs us money with insurance, etc. So we always tell anybody that it is at their own risk and at the skipper's discretion. But nobody mentioned a grand pian. If anybody complains they will be told to put it on the ferry and see how much it costs them then.'

That was the end of the piano fiasco. We finished our lime cargo on Tuesday afternoon and headed across to Portrush to load bricks for Loch Carnan.

On one occasion we were sailing up past Northbay and Eriskay. I pointed out to the mate where the SS *Politician* ran aground with her cargo of whisky and also showed the mate on the chart where the pier is on Eriskay. I then recalled a cargo we had for Eriskay and how I had once embarrassed myself.

The *Dawnlight* was in Oban to load a kit house for Eriskay but was to call in to Lochboisdale and pick up a small lorry and some tools to take round to Eriskay as well. The lorry was to be loaded at the CalMac ramp on Saturday afternoon. High water at Eriskay was six o'clock on Saturday night or 6.30, Sunday morning. I decided Saturday night's tide would do just in case the weather changed. I didn't want to be caught out in a swell with a lorry on deck. We started loading the complete building on Friday morning; concrete blocks, facing bricks, roof tiles, cement, all the plumbing stuff. Even the kitchen sink was all packed into the hold. The roofing trusses and a couple of slings of dressed timber went on deck. Both the mate and myself were pleased with the load as we didn't think we would manage to pack it all in. The lorries never seemed to stop arriving.

The trusses and timber were lashed down and we were letting the ropes go ready to sail when a car came round the pier and we were asked if we could take 20 pews out to Lochboisdale for the chapel there. I was about to refuse when the man mentioned that the office said it would be okay, if I had space for them and there would be no charge as the boat was going there anyway and it was for the church. 'Big deal!' I thought.

'Shove the lorry on the ferry. It's going to Lochboisdale and it will save double handling them,' I told him.

'No, no, you have to take them,' he said.

We loaded the pews, lashed them down and sailed. None of us were very happy about this extra cargo as we wouldn't get any thanks or even a bottle of whisky for our troubles. On Saturday afternoon we were in Lochboisdale waiting

Another kind of deck cargo. *Glenshirra* is limping into Oban with an interesting list to starboard caused by her deck cargo of logs having moved during her passage. She continued safely on her way after the cargo was re-stowed and secured. The picture illustrates the dangers to the stability of a vessel inherent in stacking weight of any sort high up on the hatch. In stormy conditions she might have capsized.

for our lorry to arrive and for someone to collect the pews. When I looked up the pier and saw a lorry sitting loaded with blocks, I said to the mate, 'Do you see that lorry with the blocks?'

'Aye,' he said.

'Wait a minute. That's the lorry that brought the pews down in Oban. I recognise that dent on the back of the trailer. They have got the pews across for nothing and sent the lorry for the blocks. I think we have been conned. They could have slipped us twenty quid at least. It's not much to ask considering we had to sling them on board and lash them and we will have to sling them onto the lorry when it arrives.'

The lorry for the pews turned up. I knew the driver quite well as he was one of the drivers that brought the seaweed down and he was always moaning about something. That day he didn't look too happy at all. He had someone helping him who didn't look as if he had done much physical work. He was wearing a dark polo neck jersey and dark trousers and looked very much like a ship's officer. The pews were covered in salt spray, which had dried. The driver moaned about this. I saw the well-dressed man looking at the dried salt on his trousers.

After much lifting and re-lifting and moaning the last three pews were being lifted onto the lorry when one slipped and hit the quay and broke one of the legs. The driver started his usual moaning. The well-dressed man shook his head. I didn't know if this was directed at me or the driver, I didn't care.

'I'll tell you what to do. Why don't the pair of you sit on one of those fuckin' pews and I will lift you up as high as I can because that is as near heaven you pair of moaning bastards will ever get.'

The lorry driver gave me a really dirty look. The well-dressed man pulled down the front of his jersey to reveal a dog collar. I felt slightly embarrassed. I reloaded the broken pew. The crew and myself went ashore and shook hands with the priest, who thanked us for delivering the pews for free and wished us many happy and safe voyages in the future.

And funnily enough, of all the puffers and small coasters I sailed on over the years, the *Dawnlight* was the one I was happiest on. So maybe delivering the pews for free and shaking hands with the priest was a good omen. I just don't know.

Our lorry for Eriskay arrived. We loaded it on deck at the ramp and caught the tide on Saturday night at Eriskay and discharged Sunday and Monday.

CHAPTER 27

A Rescue (2)

The *Dawnlight* was in Ayr and was loading coal for Castlebay on Barra. By six o'clock loading was completed. We were battened down and ready for sea, so off we went. I took the first watch down to the Mull of Kintyre. The mate took her through the Sound of Islay and when I came on at six in the morning we were north of the Sound of Islay. As it was a nice morning I decided to go west round about the north end of Colonsay and out past the Torran Rocks and set a course for the Gunna Sound. By ten o'clock we were abeam of the west rock, the most outer one of the Torran Rocks and going well. We should have been in Castlebay by four o'clock.

I heard the engine starting to race and then slowing down and then racing again and then it stopped completely. Old Bert was on holiday and I had the lobster thief on board as engineer. Charlie thought the fuel pump had packed in and there was nothing he could do as we didn't carry a spare pump. I called up Oban Radio and put a link call through to the office and told them what had happened. We required a tow and luckily the *Glenrosa* was on her way south and if I could contact her, she would come and help. Oban Radio was aware of the situation and offered to give the *Glenrosa* a call and explain what had happened and have him make his way towards us. The *Glenrosa* had received the message and turned back but wouldn't be with us for about six hours. It was then eleven o'clock.

I had spoken to the coastguard and informed them of the situation and they kept in touch. It was only a matter of waiting and hoping we didn't drift onto the rocks which we could see the waves breaking on a few miles away. By four o'clock we were drifting dangerously close to them and it was too deep to drop an anchor. I wished the *Glenrosa* would hurry. I could see her on radar but she had to go outside the west rock and back in. That made her roughly ten miles away. It was getting too close for comfort as I could see a rock breaking roughly through the sea about a mile away.

The crew had rigged a bridle by doubling two ropes together and securing it to each shoulder. We were using our longest mooring rope for a tow which was in good condition and I hoped it would do the job. The coastguard had spoken to me and I informed them of the rocks which were about a quarter of a mile away. It was half-past five and the *Glenrosa* was now about five or six minutes away. The crew were standing by with a heaving line. The *Glenrosa* arrived and picked us up. I was glad the wind hadn't picked up or it could have been serious. The *Glenrosa* towed us to Oban where the engineers changed over the fuel pump and we carried onto Castlebay arriving one day late.

From Castlebay our orders were to proceed to Lochboisdale and load dried and bagged seaweed. We loaded this and sailed for Girvan, discharged and were then to proceed to the Holy Loch for the monthly American hire. We were very happy with this as the money was good and we would probably bump into Kelly and company and have a good laugh and hear all the gossip.

Another rescue. On Christmas Day 1972, (puffermen were often required to work on national holidays), the *Raylight* suffered an engine failure in a gale off Islay. The crew were taken off by the Islay lifeboat, seen here standing by, when the anchor of the *Raylight* started to drag. The puffer was recovered, repaired and went back into service. The coxswain of the lifeboat got the RNLI Bronze Medal for the rescue. (see page 75)

CHAPTER 28

Phimister of the Mounties

It was 1979 and the Kishorn contract was finished. The coaster fleet was all renamed *Polarlight*, *Sealight*, *Raylight*, *Glenetive* and *Glenrosa* and some were in the process of having cranes and hydraulic arms fitted.

Some months earlier the company had sent all the skippers a questionnaire about what type of crane would be best suited for our type of work on the West Highland trade. I settled for a hydraulic arm because of its versatility and the different kinds of grabs that could be fitted. For example, a coal and salt grab, a block grab, a pallet jack, a timber grab. All gear that we could use for all types of cargo. The company settled for two hydraulic arms and two cranes.[20]

The *Raylight* was still gearless. Later that year she was lost in the Irish Sea whilst on passage from the Bristol Channel to Cork with a cargo of steel. The crew were saved by one of the ferries. The name *Raylight* seemed to be a bad omen for the company as both the vessels that had been so named had sunk!

As we were waiting for the Americans the crew were doing maintenance when the *Glenetive* came alongside, followed by the *Glenfyne*. Both were going on hire to the Americans as well. Faither was skipper on the *Glenetive*, John Hutton was his mate with two young boys as crew. John and Faither had sailed together for some time and were a good team. John was an ex-deep-sea man and was pretty geared up and good at his job. If they hadn't changed the regulations he would have made skipper. Kelly, Faither and John came on board the *Dawnlight* where we gave each other the usual puffer greetings. An insult here, a bit of cheek, a bit of slagging.

'I heard about you in Port Ellen, McGinn.'

'Aye, Kelly. What's this about eating the cat out in Tiree? Don't kid me that that was stew in the pot. I know you. What's cat taste like?'

'Shut up McGinn, you big bastard, I've been slagged enough about that.'

It was all harmless chat between puffermen and colleagues. Both skippers went ashore to telephone the office and John went ashore to the supermarket with one of the deckhands. I saw Kelly hand some money to John; must have been for cigarettes. A face appeared at my cabin door a while later.

'Come on, hae a dram.' It was Faither.

---

20 *Dawnlight at that time had a crane.*

'Aye, okay,' I said, thinking that we were going to the pub when they opened at eleven o'clock as it was only half past ten.

'We've a wee cairry oot. Is it okay to use your messroom? It's the biggest,' he asked.

What could I say? I already heard the voices and saw the bodies appearing.

'Let the party commence,' I said.

I hoped none of the office staff appeared. Was this a crafty move on old Faither and Kelly's part? ('We'll use McGinn's messroom and if any of the office staff arrive, McGinn will get the blame for all the drink that's on board.')

Or so they thought. Well, we would wait and see. The party was in full swing and there were about nine people in the messroom. We were into our second bottle of whisky and vodka and Faither was in his element; he had an audience and a full glass in his hand.

'Did I ever tell you about the time I got stranded in Montreal when I was just a raw deckhand and missed my ship?'

'What happened Jimmy?' I asked. The noise had quietened down a bit.

'Ah well. It was like this. A couple of ABs and myself were given shore leave and went up the town for a drink. I met this bit of stuff and went away home with her and stayed the night. I fell asleep and when I woke up it was late and I knew I was in trouble with the Captain. I paid her her money and rushed out the door and made my way to the docks to find the boat had sailed without me. Now here's me, eighteen years old and stranded in Montreal. What do I do now?' He has a drink of whisky and a mouthful of beer as if to take breath. 'Well I make my way to the agent's office to see if I can get on another ship going back to Scotland.' "No, I'm sorry son. There are no more ships this winter as the ice is closing in now. You'll just have to get a job here until the spring thaw".'

'When was this skipper?' one of Jimmy's young deckhands asked innocently.

'Aye, just after the war, 1946. September it was. Well, I wasn't going to be stuck so I makes my way to the seaman's mission to see if they can put me up for the winter and help me find a job. Well, I'm trudging along in the snow when I see this poster. "Mounted Police Wanted. Full Training Given." That's for me I say and away into the recruiting office I goes.'

"Yes, we are recruiting young men like yourself, especially if you are Scottish and from the north-east coast," the recruiting officer says. Well, here's me a stranded sailor one minute and then signed up for the Royal Canadian Mounted Police the next.'

He took another drink of whisky from his glass which had just been topped up. No mention of birth certificate, passport or seaman's ID as yet.

'Well, I did the sixteen weeks basic training. Me and this Aberdonian, and then we passed out. We drew our full uniform and were sent into the outback. A real lonely place. Nothing but snow and trees. Aye! Plenty of trees and cold, bitter cold. No wonder they needed recruits and were quick to sign us on without any questions or papers. Aye, "Scotsmen welcome" the recruiting man had said. Here's the two of us, hundreds of miles from anywhere with just our horses for company and a sack full of grub.'

The two deckhands were sitting absorbing the story. Kelly, John, myself and the rest are listening more out of good manners and respect for Faither. He carried on.

'Well, this day I'm out on patrol miles from anywhere when my horse falls into a snowdrift and I get thrown off. My horse bolts, leaving me stranded in the snow. Well, I must have walked for miles. I was becoming weaker by the minute in awful cold and didn't think I was going to make it. And hungry. I was starving by this time. I was ready for lying down and ending it when I saw this light through the trees. I staggered up to the door of this shack and just had enough strength to knock weakly on it. The door opened and this big squaw is standing there.

"What you want?" she growls.

'I'm a mounted police officer,' I reply. 'My horse bolted, I've been walking and crawling for miles. I can't go on. I'm starving of hunger.

"You eat two-day-old soup?"

'Aye! Aye missus … anything. I'm starving.'

"Okay, you come back tomorrow," and she slams the door in my face.'

I burst out laughing, as did Kelly and most of the guests. John had heard this story before. Faither's two deckhands were sitting open-mouthed and then they too saw the funny side of it. By early afternoon the party was over. Some had adjourned to the pub, some had turned in, including myself. What a man!

CHAPTER 29

'George' to the Rescue

One Friday morning in Ayr we had the shore engineers on board for a repair to the exhaust. I found out that we were to proceed to Kilroot to load salt on Saturday morning and we would be told where for, during loading. We took on bunkers. The crew went for stores. The engineers would complete the repairs that day.

By four o'clock I decided to go and see my parents who were retired and stayed in Dalrymple. They usually started loading at Kilroot at six o'clock on a Saturday, so we would sail at ten o'clock that night and instructed the crew to be on board by then. We sailed on time. The exhaust was fixed. No more watery eyes! We arrived off Kilroot at 5.30 and saw a big ship in the berth. As it was still dark I went in close to see what was happening. We were on first-name terms with the loaders and office staff.

'Keith, you are not supposed to be here. We can't load you. This big ship has to be loaded before the next high tide or she will sit on the bottom and she can't do this. She has about ten thousand tons to go,' Tommy shouted down.

Tommy went to the telephone. I lay off to wait and see what had gone wrong. It was then that I saw the small sheet of paper lying in the corner of the wheelhouse. 'Don't go to Kilroot. Proceed Portrush. Load sand for Loch Carnan. Signed, Jim.' The company must have changed the orders after I went to see my parents. The piece of paper must have blown onto the floor when I opened the wheelhouse door and in the dark I hadn't seen it. The VHF went. It was Kilroot salt sales.

'Keith we phoned your office yesterday afternoon and told them we couldn't load any boats until Monday.'

'Aye, that's right I have just found a note on the wheelhouse floor telling me to make for Portrush. I am on my way. See you next time,' I called back.

Luckily, it was just after high water and if we put 'George' on we could make about eleven knots and would be there by eleven o'clock. 'George' was a cut-down brush shaft that fitted between the wheelhouse roof and the throttle. It could push the throttle lever down and stretch the wires to the fuel pump, giving the *Dawnlight* engine an extra 50rpm. We only used 'George' in an emergency like when to get to the pub before it closed.

I was in a bit of a panic by then. Being Saturday the drivers would be on overtime and might not wait if the boat had not turned up. I put a link call through to Tommy Docherty, the harbourmaster and asked him if the drivers would wait until we arrived. All went well. We arrived at eleven and started loading. When the quarry manager arrived, I was all apologies for being late and would take the blame if there was a bill for overtime sent in. I would speak to our office on Monday and tell them I didn't see the note. I knew they wouldn't believe me. They would think I was in the pub with the crew of the *Glencloy*.

'Calm down Keith. It's okay. We have been waiting for a boat since last week. But you had that American hire to do and when I phoned up yesterday afternoon they said I could have you but would have to load you on Saturday at our expense. So don't worry. I have to pay the drivers a full shift anyway or they wouldn't come out. Can you be in Loch Carnan for Monday morning?'

'Aye, no problem. It's about twenty hours from here. We will sail right away once we load.'

Saved once again. Wow! We departed Portrush and arrived in Loch Carnan Sunday afternoon and had a quiet evening.

Loch Carnan was a fuel and Nato jetty and served the rocket range at Benbecula. The small coastal tankers arrived about once a month and topped the storage tanks. There was also a ramp for the army landing-craft, which called in with stores and equipment before carrying on out to the army base on St Kilda. The nearest shop and pub was about six miles away and was really a 'start walking and thumb a lift' job if you wanted a pint on a Sunday with no guarantee of a lift back. Nobody bothered.

Across from Loch Carnan and behind one or two small islands was an old pier called Peter's Port. The ferry had called many years ago but it had been abandoned and was in need of repair. The *Dawnlight* had loaded a cargo of scrap metal in Peters Port one weekend and was probably the last puffer to use it on a commercial basis.

We arrived on Saturday morning to find old pieces of tractors, ploughs, bits of lorries, engines, old iron wheels. Every type of scrap you could think of and all this had to be slung and lifted on board by the *Dawnlight*'s crane. What a nightmare and a mammoth task ahead of us! The scrap merchant arrived. I think he said he came from Helensburgh and he certainly could talk.

'Right boys, one hundred and fifty pounds to yourselves, cash. For helping me load. I don't have that kind of money on me just now or I would pay you in advance. But I guarantee you the money will be waiting for you when you arrive in the Rothesay dock, Glasgow. I had to draw money out of the bank yesterday to pay my hotel bill and the ferry fare. It isn't cheap living up here and to put a lorry onto the ferry. What a cost! Don't worry boys, your money's safe.'

I could hear the mate sniffling in the background and nearly reached for a hanky myself. What could we do? We just had to trust him. The loading started and so did the rain. The engineer operated the crane, the mate and two crew went ashore to sling the scrap along with the scrap merchant and his son. I went down the hold to unhook the slings and pull them free. By dinner time we were loading reasonably well. But it would take two days because of the amount of slinging and the small pieces that had to be gathered together; all physically demanding work and in continuous rain. We worked until seven o'clock on Saturday night and had about two-thirds of the cargo loaded.

The scrap merchant wanted us to work on using our lights and he used his lorry lights. We told him and his son to do the impossible and stop for the night. We were all absolutely knackered with all the scrambling amongst the scrap, trying to put slings through, making sure pieces didn't fall out; all very sore on the legs. We had our evening meal and just like Loch Carnan there was nowhere to go, so were heading for our bunks when the scrappy arrived.

'Come on boys, I'll take you up to the pub for a drink and run you back down again.'

I didn't go, but the four crew were all in favour and I heard them returning about one in the morning. Sunday dawned bright and clear. The rain had stopped. The crew were up and ready to start.

'Keith, you missed yourself last night. He wouldn't let us buy a drink. He must have bought about seven or eight rounds. He took us back to his caravan and had a few more drinks and a pile of sandwiches and sausage rolls. Aye, he is alright this guy, we'll get our money in Glasgow okay.'

We finished the loading, battened down and sailed. The scrap merchant letting our ropes go.

'See you in the Rothesay dock on Tuesday,' he shouted.

We never saw him again and never got paid a penny. Well, at least the crew got a few drinks and a sandwich. When I mentioned to the company that we hadn't been paid, thinking that they might have been able to get our money, I was met with the response.

'Nothing to do with us. You took the loading on, you should have made sure you got your money.'

'Aye, up you as well!' I thought.

CHAPTER 30

Hogged

We finished our Loch Carnan cargo and sailed out past Peters Port bound for Keose, where we picked up our cargo of seaweed and sailed for Girvan. After Girvan it was up to Ayr to load coal for Broadford on Skye. And then it happened. Catastrophe!

We loaded our cargo and sailed in time to catch high water at Broadford, which was at eight o'clock in the morning. We arrived to find a coaster in the outside berth and had no choice but to go ahead of him and discharge there. I kept our stern tight under the coaster's bow so as not to dry out too much as part of that cargo was for Raasay as well. We hoped to sail at dinner time the next day.

We discharged away quite merrily all day with the Dawnlight sitting on the bottom at low water and refloating again by half flood about five o'clock. We finished for the day shortly after. The next morning the discharge started, everything was going to plan and if the tide stayed up for a while we would have managed to sail before we took the bottom. We had cleared out the after end and I was digging out under the crane, which was fixed in the middle of the hatch when the grab caught one of the sealing boards and pulled it out.

'Oh hell,' I thought. What had happened?

The boards were a tight fit, the grab very rarely gripped one when it was closing. Something was wrong. The crew cleared a space with their shovels and found that the boards all across the hold had popped. It could only mean one thing. The Dawnlight had sat on something at low water. She was hogged.

We cleared out the cargo that was for Broadford and proceeded round to Raasay and discharged the coal there. The sealing boards were a mess. It was very serious. Though the Dawnlight was not leaking she had broken her back. I was gutted and didn't know what to tell the office. We finished discharging in Raasay and as it was near low water, sailed back round to Broadford to see if we could see anything lying on the bottom.

'Oh please, let it be an old pile or a big stone that has come out from the side of the pier,' I kept saying to myself.

The coaster had sailed, so we lay at the front and had a look at the berth we had been in. The ebb tide hadn't gone back far enough so we could not see anything unusual. No piles or big stones lying on the bottom, just sand and weed. The beach didn't look level though. It seemed to go deeper quite quickly where

111

our stern was. There was nothing more we could do, so I plucked up courage and telephoned the company. There were not too happy with the report I gave them and ordered the *Dawnlight* back to Ayr, so that the marine and engineer superintendents could assess the damage. It was not looking good. I told the crew I was in trouble. I was no longer number one son.

We sailed from Broadford and on passing Kyle spotted the *Glencloy* lying there and spoke to the skipper on the VHF and told him what had happened. He confirmed my worst fears. There was a ledge of rock that stretched out two thirds of the way up the pier and was quite often covered by sand so you couldn't see it at low water. In the old days when Broadford was quite a busy port the old puffermen had a white mark painted on the pier to show where it was. You had to go ahead of the mark at high water to avoid sitting on the outcrop of rock. As ferry and puffer trade declined over the years nobody had any need to go to the inside berth, so the paint mark and local knowledge faded away.

He also told me it must have been years since two cargo vessels arrived in Broadford at the same time and of course, with me not knowing the outcrop was there and trying to keep the *Dawnlight* floating for a quick getaway, sat slap bang in the middle of it. How unlucky can one get?

'I hate these bloody puffers, I should have left when I came back from Tiree when I was deckhand fourteen years ago. Oh well, I suppose it will be up to the office for tea and biscuits maybe.'

What was it one skipper once said? 'If you have been a bad boy and are ordered up to the office, always remember if you are kept waiting, but are offered tea and biscuits, it's not too serious. Tea alone, no biscuits: quite serious. No tea or biscuits and ignored, you are in big trouble.'

We arrived safely back in Ayr. The marine and engineer superintendents came on board and totally ignored me and checked the hold and engine mountings. I heard them talking between themselves on deck. The engineer super went ashore. The marine super came into the wheelhouse.

'This is bloody serious, Keith. This boat is wrecked. I don't know if she is worth repairing. It is going to cost thousands. You have run ashore somewhere. You and your crew are bloody lucky you didn't lose your lives. Now where did you run aground?'

'But Captain, I have told the truth. We sat on an outcrop of rock at Broadford on the inside berth. There was a coaster using the normal berth. I didn't know anything about a rock. Ask the skipper of the Glencloy.' I tried to explain.

'Right, take your boat up to Greenock. We'll dry dock her and soon see if you are telling the truth. If there are deep score marks on her bottom, she has run ashore. I want a full written report on this and where is your log book? I want to see what you have written in it.'

On the way down to Ayr I had filled in a written report on exactly what happened, giving high and low waters and also part of what the skipper of the

Glencloy had said. Next day in Greenock I went ashore and telephoned the office, expecting an invitation for tea and biscuits. Nothing serious happened, which made me feel worse. The personnel manager, who seemed to be the only person who wanted to talk to me said, 'Keith, this could not have happened at a worse time for the company. With the cost of the new cranes for the bigger boats and now this, can you phone back in the afternoon?'

The shore fitters and engineer super were on board and didn't say very much. Oh well, there was not much I could do about it. Everybody seemed to think I had run aground somewhere, which was wrong. By late afternoon the marine super was on board.

'Right, you have to go to Oban and relieve the skipper of the Glencloy for a month. There is a train leaves Glasgow about six o'clock. Be on it.'

I looked at the wheelhouse clock and if I rushed about like an idiot I could catch it.

'No, I am not going to Oban tonight. I am having a night at home first and will travel tomorrow night, okay.'

It was time to sort things out one way or another. The accident to the *Dawnlight* was a genuine mistake. There was a long pause.

'Aye, okay then. Phone the office and let them know,' the super said.

I knew the heat was off, so I went ashore and telephoned, to be told that the *Glencloy* had been held up and wouldn't be in Oban until the next afternoon and, yes, have a night at home and give them a ring from the house before I left for Oban. This was a great weight off my shoulders.

I travelled to Oban on the evening train and met the skipper of the *Glencloy* who told me the office had asked him about the outcrop of rock at Broadford and he had told them the same as he had told me on the VHF. Things worked out okay. I felt bad about the damage but just didn't know that outcrop was there. I did a month on the *Glencloy* and then had two weeks leave and by that time the company decided to repair the *Dawnlight*. I rejoined her in Greenock and took her into the dry-dock. As soon as they drained the dock I shot down to the dock bottom where the two supers were examining her hull. Not a scrape or score anywhere. The hull pushed up but not a mark.

'Yes!' I felt like shouting. 'You pair didn't believe me when I said I hadn't run aground.'

I just climbed out of the dock and went back on board.

CHAPTER 31

Wedding Bells

At one time there was a young mate called Angus on the *Glenfyne* who hailed from Benbecula. He had been deepsea and had worked on the North Sea supply boats before he came to the puffers. He was a good hand, we all liked him and he fitted in well.

Tobermory was a good stopping off place for shelter if the weather was too rough for crossing the Minch or going round Ardnamurchan. During one of the *Glenfyne*'s visits Angus met a young woman called Fiona in her 20s, about his own age. As she came from his neighbouring island of North Uist and like him spoke the Gaelic, they became friends and soon were going steady. They saw each other whenever the *Glenfyne* was in Tobermory and Angus phoned whenever he could. But on his visits to Tobermory his courting never got past a few kisses and cuddles and try as he would he could not get Fiona to go any further.

'No. Not till we're married,' was the usual response.

This went on every time the *Glenfyne* was in and poor Angus was becoming cross-eyed with frustration. So he decided to try a different tack and asked Fiona to marry him.

'Yes! Yes!' was the eager reply. 'I will marry you.'

Angus was delighted and thought their love would be consummated. However the response was the same.

'No. No. Not until we are married. It wouldn't be right.'

Angus was fed up with this courting lark as he had just forked out for the price of an engagement ring.

Word of this soon got round the puffer fleet and everybody had a good laugh at Angus's predicament. He seriously was considering going back deepsea or back to the supply boats and giving the marriage lark a miss. He was moaning about his fate one day in the messroom when the skipper said, 'I could do the marriage ceremony.' The engineer fell about laughing and said, 'How the hell can you marry them? You're not qualified. You don't even have a proper slipper's ticket.'

In all his wisdom, and that was why he was skipper, the skipper replied, 'I know that. You know that. But Fiona doesn't know that. She's not too bright. He's no intention of marrying her he just wants to get her into bed.'

'She's not too bad,' Angus chips in, 'she speaks good Gaelic and can write it as well. But I don't know if I really want to marry her. Anyway, as Charlie says, you are really not qualified and I don't think even deepsea captains are allowed to marry couples these days.'

'I've found an old almanack in the cabin there and it has the captain's guide and the verse to perform the ceremony. Buy a cheap wedding ring and I'll read out the words. We could make it look real. She'll think it's her lucky day getting a husband like you. Tell her you will send her your wages to set up home and she will be putty in your hands.'

The *Glenfyne* was not in the north for a while so Angus did not see Fiona for about six weeks after they got engaged. The ship was due for her Loadline Certificate and an engine overhaul and was due to be in Ayr for a few days if not longer.

'Here's an idea,' said the skipper, 'why don't you see if Fiona can get time off and bring her to Ayr. She can stay on board and you remember what we were talking about in Kyle?'

Fiona duly arrived in Ayr and Angus met her at the station. During the walk to the Ship Inn at the harbour (no taxis for the bold Angus) he sweet-talked her into agreeing to the wedding. Whether she actually believed that a puffer skipper could marry them is doubtful. She was probably more worried about losing Angus and the prospect of his weekly wage for home-making.

They celebrated in the Ship Inn, bought a large carry-out and staggered on board the *Glenfyne*. With the help of an old wedding ring (the property of the skipper's girlfriend Jean from a previous marriage), with a deckhand as best man and with Jean as bridesmaid, the skipper performed the marriage ceremony. The carry-out was consumed, a good laugh was had all round and everybody staggered off to their own cabins.

All had hangovers on the Sunday morning except Angus who had a cheery grin on his face and Fiona who seemed neither up nor down. She had to leave later in the day to get the first ferry from Oban to Craignure on the Monday morning to get back to her job in Tobermory. The honeymoon was a short one. Angus walked her to the station and Fiona waved a tearful farewell. Angus promised a proper honeymoon later when he got the chance. He would phone often and write regularly.

A fortnight later Fiona phoned the company office and demanded to now where her husband was and why she had not been sent any wages.

'I didn't know Angus was married and who are you anyway?' said the voice at the Glasgow end of the phone, not having a clue what she was talking about.

'I am Angus's wife. We were married on board the Glenfyne by the skipper just over two weeks ago and I haven't heard from him since.'

'Married! By the skipper? I might have known he would be involved somehow. Listen, dear, our skippers don't have the authority to marry anybody. It's not legal. You've been taken in.'

Meanwhile Angus had left the employment of Glenlight and gone back deepsea. Nothing more was ever said about the wedding but the story went round the fleet.

Fiona married a fisherman from Lewis a few months later and five months after that had a son who she called John Angus after her husband. Funnily enough her son looked exactly like her new husband. Somebody on the puffers worked back the dates and decided that the 'Not until we are married' bit was quite true, although perhaps it might have been in Angus's case. One observant pufferman noticed that the Lewis fishing boat had been working out of Tobermory the whole year. It looked like she had been two-timing Angus when she married him. Maybe she was just keeping her options open.

A few months later one of the lads met Angus in Queen Street station and told him about Fiona marrying the Lewis fisherman.

'Would that be John Angus from Stornaway ? Och! He's a full cousin of mine. We sometimes get mistaken for brothers.'

Angus boarded his train and left us all guessing.

CHAPTER 32

The Polarlight

The *Dawnlight* was repaired and started trading again. Shortly after that I left her and joined the *Polarlight*. She was a fine wee boat the *Dawnlight* and I have a lot of happy memories of her but cash is king and the bigger boats were getting the cream of the cargoes. It was about this time, the early 80's, that the *Glencloy* was sold[21] and the *Pibroch* took over the American hire. This left the *Dawnlight*, *Glenfyne*, *Sealight*, *Polarlight*, *Glenetive* and *Glenrosa* trading on the West Coast.

Another tragic accident had happened sometime after the *Glencloy* had been sold. The crew had transferred to the *Sealight*. The skipper[22] was boarding one afternoon when he slipped and fell between the ship and the pier. Some workmen were passing and saw what had happened but were too late to save the old skipper, who died in the ambulance. It was another sad loss of a very experienced man who had spent a lifetime at sea. He was a skipper who took pride in his commands and kept them clean and tidy. Tragic.

By the end of 1980 I had been on the *Polarlight* for about six months. The old puffer way of life was changing; more rules and regulations were in force. Proper log books had to be kept, lifeboat drills, fire fighting drills had to be carried out and everybody had to have certificates. The skippers and mates were issued certificates of service, provided they had done the relevant job for a number of years.

As the boats were becoming bigger it was not so easy to slip alongside a pier for a night ashore and also because of the bigger tonnage, harbour and pier dues were becoming more expensive. So the company started complaining when bills arrived for dues when we had only called in on the way past for some food, etc. One skipper, when pulled up about his extra visits, made the excuse that he couldn't drop his anchors because the windlass was seized.

About a fortnight later he arrived in Ayr to load a cargo of coal. The shore engineers were waiting for him. They came on board with their burning gear, grease guns and found the windlass and anchors had nothing wrong with them. All were free. An invitation was given to the skipper to come to the head office for

21 *Autumn 1979. She was 14 years old at this stage and with four 350-tonners then in the fleet she was excess to cargo-carrying capacity.*
22 *Kai Dalberg Andersen. He had fled to Scotland from his native Denmark when it was over-run by the Nazis in World War II. After over 40 years of service to West Highland shipping in the puffer trade he was awarded the MBE.*

tea and biscuits, where he was shown bills for all the ports he had called into over the past six months. The non-cargo ones shown in red with the appropriate costs. Within a couple of days the rest of us knew about his visit to the office.

'Did you get biscuits with your tea?' someone asked.

'Oh aye, two chocolate digestives on a plate, they were a bit soft though. As if they had been lying in a damp place for a long time. I ate half of one and said I wasn't really that hungry. I got the usual lecture about costs and about how much the harbour dues come to every year for all the boats and we'd have to stop calling into the likes of Tobermory and Campbeltown, unless we have a cargo for these places or need repairs. I think everybody is to receive a letter about this. The job's not the same. Anyway I tapped them for a sub on my way out, so that hasn't changed.'

The coaster fleet were trading further afield. As far down as New Ross on the south coast of Ireland where we picked up malting barley for Islay. By 1983–4 the timber trade was in full swing, with cargoes of three-metre pulpwood for Ardyne, sawn logs for Girvan and Belfast and two-metre pulp wood for Workington. The paper mill at Workington made light, high-quality cardboard for the tobacco and cereal industry and was to become a regular run over the next seven or eight years. With the loss of the old skipper and old Faither thinking of retiring, Davie Langlands and Kelly, Tommy Ferguson, Willie Cowie and myself were left as the last of the original small boatmen.

In 1975 Glenlight Shipping Ltd bought four 400-tonne sister ships for the West Highland trade and this picture of MV *Wib* illustrates their general characteristics. Unfortunately they had no cargo gear but were adapted to take travelling gantry cranes on deck. When these were fitted they could carry 340 tons of cargo, 100 tons more than the *Dawnlight/Glenfyne* class. Two were named 'Glens'; Etive and Rosa and two 'lights'; Sea and Polar and so the naming traditions of Ross & Marshall and Hay-Hamilton were continued.

The *Polarlight* had an hydraulic arm fitted on a travelling gantry and we were starting to load timber cargoes along with the usual salt and coal. The idea was to load salt or coal north to the islands and pick up timber on the way south for Ardyne where the timber was bundled and banded into six-tonne packages. It was then shipped to Sweden by bigger vessels where it was turned into paper and then shipped back across to British ports, etc.

With the puffer fleet dying out and with the introduction of bigger vessels, they weren't puffers anymore, rather small coasters and with fewer vessels on the coast the nights and weekends in port became fewer. The old way of life was dying out. Everything became more serious with the company pushing more and more for greater productivity.

The *Polarlight* loaded a cargo of 330 tonnes of coal in Ayr for Carbost on Skye. We arrived in Carbost at six o'clock in the morning and had just finished opening the steel hatches and were just connecting the grab when I saw the lights of a lorry appearing in the distance coming towards the pier. The lorry was for us so we were starting the discharge by seven o'clock. By seven o'clock that night we were closing the hatches and making ready for sea again, having finished the cargo in about eleven hours. I remembered back to the *Lady Isle* in 1967 when we had a full cargo of 130 tons for Carbost. It took us one-and-a-half days with shovels or about 14 hours to complete the discharge. That was how fast things had changed in 15 years.

If you are ever in Carbost and tied up at the pier, on the cliff face there is an underground spring running through the cliff into a small man-made pool. The water is the sweetest and coldest I have ever tasted, even on the hottest of days. It is always ice-cold and in a glass of Talisker seems to add to the flavour. Lovely!

MV *Polarlight*, the author's first command in the 400-tonne class. She was fitted with a travelling hydraulic crane, here seen picking up sawn logs from the pier at Ardrishaig.

CHAPTER 33

'Passengers'

The *Lady Morven* had just finished discharging in Brodick one Saturday morning. Her young skipper and crew were in the pub having a few beers prior to sailing, when they were approached by a farmer who asked them if it was possible to take half-a-dozen cows round to the Holy Isle for him. The skipper, a man who could smell a pound a mile off quickly agreed and a price was fixed. No thought was given about how they were going to tackle the job. The deckhand was a man who had worked on farms for years before going to sea and had a good idea that this might be more difficult than it looked.

'Emm … how do we get the cows on board, skipper? And, how do we get them ashore again?'

'Oh! They are very tame. We could sling them on board and do the same at the Holy Isle. Just go in as close as you can to the beach and put the sling on and lower them over the side, unhook the sling and they will swim ashore. I've seen photos of horses and ponies being loaded on board the ferries with slings, so it should work the same way with cattle. Easy, nothing to it,' the farmer replied.

He went off to fetch the cows. The crew remained and had a few more drinks, so were in fine fettle when the cows arrived. The deckhand, being an ex-farm hand, decided he had better help the farmer to sling the animals. The cattle float was brought as near to the side of the pier as possible, the derrick was swung out ready for the first lift. The cattle had been tethered to the side of the float so were all facing forward.

The deckhand passed the end of the sling under the belly of the first cow. The sling was broad and was the proper item for the job and must have been used for this purpose many years before. He was on his knees adjusting the sling so the cow wouldn't be injured and could be lifted straight up when the cow directly in front of him decided to relieve itself and let rip. The deckhand who wasn't too sober anyway, tried to scramble clear but wasn't quick enough and got covered in watery cow shit. The skipper, mate and farmer were pissing themselves laughing and the deckhand was cursing and swearing to the high heavens, all of which made the cows nervous and fidgety.

The farmer saw this and asked for everybody to calm down. The deckhand went away to change himself. The cows were eventually loaded but were in a pretty nervous condition and were bellowing loudly by the time they reached the

Holy Isle. The farmer didn't go with the crew so they were left on their own to reverse the procedure and make sure the cows got ashore safely.

On reaching the Holy Isle the drink was starting to wear off, and the skipper began to realise that the easy money was not so easy after all. They had six cows in the hold. They had been paid. There were only the three of them and they hadn't tethered the cows before sailing so they were wandering about the hold bellowing madly and were very agitated. An argument started up about who was brave enough to enter the hold and try and sling them. The deckhand refused. He had already had to change himself. The mate said he was not doing it. The skipper said he had to watch the boat didn't go aground and it was not his job.

They decided they would have a can of beer or two, stop the engine and see if the cows would calm down a bit. After about an hour or so the six cows seemed to have settled. The mate and deckhand had swallowed a few beers and regained their courage and would go into the hold and sling the animals. The skipper would lower them into the water and take the sling off.

The puffer didn't seem to have drifted too far off the island, so they didn't start the main engine in case the noise upset the cows. All was going well. The first two cows had been slung and lowered into the water with the first one swimming towards the Holy Isle and the second one following. The third one had been slung and was being lowered into the water when the skipper looked towards the island. The first two cows were swimming the other way, making for the fields on Arran. The crew had three cows in the water and three in the hold and would now have to go and turn the first two.

It must have been the first time in history that a puffer and her crew had to round up cattle and head them in the right direction. They managed to turn the first two by steaming in close to them and shouting and waving and eventually got them ashore on the island. The third cow, by then, was swimming towards Lamlash and also had to be turned. The Wild West had reached Arran. You ain't seen nothing until you see a puffer herding cows, especially if you knew the skipper and crew as I did. Only the stetsons were missing.

After a struggle and more herding, all six cows arrived safely on the Holy Isle where their descendents are probably still there to this day. The poor crew had a lot of cleaning up to do and the smell of cow dung and urine lingered aboard for weeks.

About a year prior to my transfer from the *Dawnlight* to the *Polarlight*, I was returning to the *Dawnlight* one Sunday morning after having a couple of nights at home. The *Dawnlight* was in Ayr loaded with coal for Portree on Skye which was a 22-hour run, so I had said to the crew we would sail at nine o'clock on the Sunday morning. Sitting on the wall across from the bus stop was a noted worthy; a friend of mine who informed me I had just missed a bus and there wouldn't be another one for an hour. This was about 6.45 in the morning. It meant that I was going to be late on board. Something I didn't like to be. John had just been for the Sunday papers and was enjoying the early morning sunshine.

'Why don't you get old Dick, your father-in-law, to run you to Ayr?'

'Good idea. I'll go round and wake him up,' I said.

John decided to come for the run, after we eventually got old Dick out of his bed. John still had the Sunday papers under his arm. On the way to Ayr, he mentioned he wouldn't mind coming for a sail sometime.

'Why don't you come now? There is a spare bunk. Plenty of clean laundry. I'll give you a towel and razor. Can't help you with a change of clothes though.'

'Aye, okay. Dick, will you tell Minnie I've gone to Portree with Keith and will be back next weekend?'

'No problem, I'll just go round to your house when I get back,' said Dick. John and myself went on board.

John still had the Sunday papers. The crew were all there. We let go and sailed on time. About two o'clock the *Dawnlight* was just north of the Mull of Kintyre when Portpatrick radio came on with traffic for the *Dawnlight*. It was my wife calling. I immediately thought that there had been an accident or something was wrong at home.

'Keith, is old John with you? Minnie is about off her head with worry. He left the house just after six this morning to go for the papers and has never returned. Over.'

'Aye, John's here. Did old Dick not go round to the house and tell Minnie that he was going for a sail? Over.'

'I didn't know my Dad was involved in this. I thought you were going by bus to Ayr. You should know better than to trust him to deliver messages. John should have telephoned from Ayr and stopped his wife from worrying, or you could have put a link call through and told me. I would have told Minnie. Minnie called to the door thinking John was here as she had tried Soddy's, Wee Rab's and Biff's and was about to phone the hospital. You were our last hope. When will you be back in the Clyde? Over.'

'Tell Minnie we will be back in Ayr on Wednesday afternoon. John should be home Wednesday night. Over.'

'Aye, okay. See you later. Gone.'

Portpatrick ended the call. We carried on. John enjoyed the sail up through the sounds, past Mull, Ardnamurchan with the Small Isles and the Cuillins on our port side with the sun just setting on the horizon over the Outer Isles, a really beautiful sight on a clear summer's night. We arrived in Portree on time and had the boat ready for discharging by eight o'clock. But no lorries appeared. The harbourmaster arrived and told me there was a tanker due at nine o'clock and that I would have to clear off and go to anchor until he finished discharging, which would take five or six hours. That was a day lost. We would not finish until Wednesday. John wasn't too worried. He was enjoying himself.

We eventually got started on Tuesday morning and finished on Wednesday afternoon arriving back in Ayr on Thursday. John and I jumped on a bus and headed for home. Getting off the bus I noticed that John still had the Sunday papers even though we had all read them and it was then Thursday. Strange, I thought. Of course, John suggested that we had some light refreshments before proceeding home and adjourned to our local. John got slagged the minute he walked through the pub door.

'Oh, the wanderer returns! We're not sending you for the Sunday papers. Where were you? Wait till Minnie gets her hands on you.'

'I was away on a Hebridean cruise with my good friend here. You are only jealous. We went to Portree and then back to Ayr.'

The jungle telegraph was beating because Minnie appeared about five minutes later and was not a happy person. John, quick as a flash said,

'Oh, hello dear. I was just on my way home with the Sunday papers. Did you keep my breakfast for me? I know you like to read the Broons and Oor Wullie.'

'I'll bloody Sunday papers you, this is Thursday. The fright you gave me. If it hadn't been for Jo, Keith's wife, I wouldn't have known where you were you were, you bloody old fool you.'

Minnie calmed down and had a drink. Everybody had a good laugh. John enjoyed his sail and talked about it a few times over the years.

CHAPTER 34

'The Office'

Sometimes the office staff got it wrong or didn't inform each other on what the boats were doing. On one occasion two boats were sent to Corpach in the Caledonian Canal for the same cargo. One boat came from the north and one up from the south. Both arrived and locked into the Corpach Basin within an hour of each other. The skipper who arrived first thought the other was heading through the canal.

'Are you for Inverness?' he asked.

'No, we're to load bricks for Loch Carnan. What are you loading?' asked the new arrival.

'We're here to load bricks, there must be a hulluva lot of bricks going to Loch Carnan.'

They both had a good idea something was wrong and went to the telephone.

'Who gave you your orders?' said one skipper to the other.

'John. Who gave you yours?' he replied.

'Jim, why?'

'They both sit across the room from each other and don't tell each other where they are sending the boats. The right hand doesn't know what the left is doing. What a shower!'

It was a bad mistake by the company. The boat that was south could have loaded salt north. The brick company was putting pressure on and the shipping company didn't want to lose the cargo. The freight rate on bricks was better than salt. In the hurry one cargo manager didn't tell the other what he was doing and two boats landed in the same port for the same cargo. The new arrival locked back out and went for seaweed. When the news spread round the fleet it was a good morale boost as the office 'never made mistakes', according to them! It was always the skipper to blame if things went wrong.

On another occasion the *Polarlight* was in Portree discharging salt. When I went to the telephone for our orders, they were to proceed back to Kilroot to load salt for north again but to give the office a ring late in the afternoon and let them know if I would be finished in time to load the next afternoon at Kilroot without incurring overtime. On returning to the telephone I got the other cargo manager who said,

'Oh son. I don't know what to do with you. Are you about finished?'

'Aye, the crew are just closing the hatches now,' I said.

'I have a cargo of coal in Ayr to be shifted. The salt people are screaming for boats. Portrush have road chips to be shifted. Glenarm have been on, they have a cargo of lime chippings for Ayr. I don't know where to send you first. The other boats are all busy. Can you give the office a ring sharp nine tomorrow morning and don't go south of the Mull of Kintyre before contacting us. Whoever shouts loudest gets the boat.'

We set sail from Portree and by five in the morning were the in Sound of Islay. I didn't know whether to head for the Mull in case it was Ayr or Kilroot or head for Rathlin on the off-chance it might have been Red Bay or Portrush. Rathlin won. I slowed down and we were just north of the Mull and Rathlin at nine o'clock when I put a link call through.

'Okay son. Can you make Portrush in time to load today?'

'Aye. Nae bother. Telephone the quarry and let the harbourmaster know as well. We will be ready to load on arrival.'

We finished loading in Portrush and I went to the telephone and spoke to the other cargo manager. The one I spoke to in the morning in Portree.

'Okay. That's us loaded. We will be sailing shortly.'

'Oh that's great, Keith. You must have had a good run down.

'We are not at Kilroot. We are in Portrush for a cargo of road chips for Loch Carnan. We have just finished loading.'

'Bloody hell! You're supposed to be in Kilroot. Not Portrush. Who told you to go there?'

'I was told to make a call to the office at nine o'clock this morning and was given instructions to proceed to Portrush and load road chips for Loch Carnan.'

'Right! Phone me back later.'

The telephone went dead. The boat was loaded and Loch Carnan was where we were headed. As I left the harbourmaster's office I met the quarry manager and told him we weren't supposed to be there, according to one cargo manager.

'I phoned John at his house last night and more or less demanded a boat. This cargo has been ready for a couple of weeks. They are waiting for it out in Loch Carnan. It's to finish off the new causeway. So he said you would be in the area and would send you today.'

It was another case of one manager not telling the other what was happening or changing the orders and not letting on.

CHAPTER 35

The New Glencloy

The *Polarlight*, *Sealight*, *Glenrosa* and *Glenetive* all had MacGregor[23] hatches, so life was a lot easier for the crews. No wooden hatches to throw on and canvas covers to pull on in a gale of wind, with wedges to be hammered in. The ships all had autopilots so there was no standing for hours behind a wheel unless the autopilot broke down. The accommodation, however, was a bit cramped. The skipper had a small cabin, as had the mate. The two crew had a two-bunk cabin. All four shared the shower and washroom on a first-come, first-served basis; no pecking order. As the lighting system was 24-volt, we had no washing machine or freezer, just a small caravan fridge. We had a really good gas cooker, which made a lot of difference. We always had plenty of clean laundry; sheets, pillow cases, blankets, etc, on board, as most of the regular ports had a ship's laundry service which could do a one-day service. The heating on the four boats was by diesel stove which sometimes cut out, usually in the middle of the night. In all honesty, they were comfortable boats to live on.

The trading pattern was changing and after the miner's strike in 1984 shipments of coal from Ayr to the islands virtually stopped. The coasters were having to head south to Glasson Dock, a small port between Fleetwood and Heysham, and Garston on the River Mersey to pick up any coal cargoes. There were no more odd nights at home. It was sad knowing that you were only about six hours from home but having to carry on south to load the coal that would normally have been loaded in Ayr on Monday morning.

Another run we did was down the West Coast of Ireland to load seaweed from Burtonport, Westport and Kilkieran. All the coasters got a wee shot at this. In the winter this was a nightmare of a run due to the high Atlantic swell that could get up. From Tory Island to Erris Head across Donegal Bay was about a 14-hour run. Nobody liked doing the run and if we could make an excuse to get out of it, we would.

I was lucky. In the six years I was on the *Polarlight* I went to Kilkieran twice. Kilkieran is a small port just north of the Aran Islands in Galway Bay and is the

---

23 *These were steel hatches that folded up when they were opened. They were pulled open and shut by the vessel's winch. These ships also had double bottoms for water ballast. This was taken on when they were lightship to make passages easier.*

The last *Glencloy*, (the fifth to bear the name) is seen here discharging at Corpach near the southern end of the Caledonian Canal. Ben Nevis can be seen in the background. Glenlight Shipping, in its search for economy of scale, bought the 600-tonne deadweight *Sea Maas* for conversion for the West Highland trade. The gantry crane that was fitted can be seen operating a conventional grab at the forward end of the hold. She was the author's last command in the puffer trade.

most southerly port where the seaweed was loaded. This was then taken to Barcaldine, near Oban.

We left Oban one winter on the 2nd February, bound for Kilkieran. By Saturday 4th, my birthday, we had only reached Lough Swilly and were lying at anchor awaiting a moderation in the weather. The forecast for Sunday was southwest veering west or northwest five to seven, occasionally gale eight. No use us trying to get round Tory Island in that. On the Monday the forecast was still the same. The swell was running up the Lough and we were rolling about quite a bit, which was pretty uncomfortable. I put a link call through to the office to report our position and bleat about the weather, hoping they might change the orders. No such luck! We still had to go as soon as we received a notice of the weather moderating.

We upped anchor and dropped it again off Rathmullen on the Monday afternoon. This made it more comfortable. The Thursday afternoon forecast was giving a decrease in wind strength. I decided to wait another 18 hours and go out and have a look and see what the swell was like in daylight. We slipped alongside Rathmullen Pier and picked up some stores; bread, butcher meat, etc. By seven o'clock on Friday morning we had upped anchor and were proceeding down

Loch Swilly. The wind had dropped completely. The barometer was rising slowly which was a good sign. By the time we reached the open sea there was a huge swell running but no white tops and nothing breaking. One minute we were on the crest of a wave and could see for miles, the next we were running down hill and could see nothing but water all round us, and blue sky above. I was glad we had changed the fuel filters and cleaned the header tank while we were at anchor. I would have hated for something to have gone wrong at that time. The horrendous swell carried on for the next three to four hours but by the time we reached Tory Island, it had died away to a moderate Atlantic swell which we carried all the way to Erris Head. We made it in time to load on Saturday and then lost a day as another small depression passed over.

We sailed on Mondays' tide and arrived in Barcaldine on Thursday morning. It was 14 days since we left Oban. One cargo and one freight in two weeks! Not much profit in that. I hoped I wouldn't get any more of these horrible runs, especially in the winter and the short daylight. It makes me shiver when I think about it.

By Christmas 1985 rumours were rife about the company buying a bigger coaster but nothing definite was being said by the office. The *Polarlight* was in Ayr loading fertiliser for Broadford on Skye when the Bell Ringer appeared on board.

'Where are you going?' I asked.

'You are going on leave. I have come to relieve you.'

'First, I have heard nothing about that. Did they say why? I don't think I have done anything wrong.'

What had I been up to that had caught their attention? I hadn't asked for leave. It was only the middle of January. I signed Davie on and myself off and filled out the log book in and gave Davie the run-down of fuel on board, oil, filters, etc. One of the shore fitters came round.

'You have to come to the office and phone the boss, Keith.'

It turned out the company were interested in a bigger vessel and were going to have a look at it and wanted me to go with them. I had to keep this to myself meantime. We flew down to Hull and had a look at the vessel called the *Sea Maas*. She was a sound-looking vessel of about 750 tonnes deadweight and had a large cubic capacity, which would be ideal for timber. I was asked if I would go skipper her if the company decided to buy it. By May the company had purchased the *Sea Maas* and renamed her *Glencloy*.[24]

This did not go down well with one of my fellow skippers. He remarked to my mate one day,

'There is only one thing wrong with the new *Glencloy*.'

'Aye, what's that skipper?'

---

24 *This was the fifth vessel to carry this name since it had first been used by G&G Hamilton in 1895 when they built a wooden puffer in the Cloy Burn on Arran.*

'That bastard, McGinn got her instead of me.'

Of course the mate came right back and told me what he had said. After that I used to wind him up anytime we were having a drink together. I would say to him, 'You're good skipper, really good. But as long as I am around, you will always be second-best.'

The skipper would be hopping mad at this and call me all kinds of names. Some people have no sense of humour.

From June 1986 and for the next six years, the *Glencloy* was kept busy running timber from the West Coast of Scotland to places such as Belfast, Workington, Birkenhead, Ayr and Ardrossan. Coal went from Garston to Stornoway, salt from Kilroot to various highland ports and fertiliser from Cork and Arklow to Ayr. A lot of nautical miles were covered in a year. The amount of cargoes moved was about the same as the puffers of 20 years past, about 95 per year. The *Glencloy*, with her hydraulic arm,[25] designed for speed loading and discharging, could unload salt, provided there were plenty of lorries, at about 90 tonnes per hour. So a one-day discharge was normal. Arrive in the morning and sail again that evening; it was the same with timber: sail through the night, crew load and sail that evening. But the fun had gone out of the job and there were few characters or worthies left.

I had occasion to pick up a pilot for a certain port south of the Mull of Galloway and to this day I don't know what had upset him. He started mouthing off about the puffermen and how we were just a load of no-use drunks who wouldn't get a job in a real company. He was really being nasty and if it hadn't been for the fact I needed him on board, I would have decked him, pilot or not.

I waited until he calmed down a bit and asked him how many ports he piloted vessels into. Only two, was his reply, the one we were going to and one other, both with leading lights and a buoyed channel, so they were both straightforward.

'You know pilot, in the course of twenty odd years a pufferman may visit about one hundred and fifty ports. He doesn't take a pilot anywhere unless it is compulsory. He could be in one port this week and may not be back for a year or maybe two years. He is still expected to remember such things as the chimney on the end house in line with the big rock on the shore keeps you clear of the submerged rock at the entrance. Or the tree with the low branches in line with end of the pier takes you right up the centre of the channel keeping you in deep water.

'All this handed down from pufferman to pufferman, over the years. You wouldn't survive on the West Coast of Scotland with your an attitude. The puffermen would blank you out. I know most of us take a good drink, but we still shift a lot of cargo over a year. We are not all that bad. At least we are open about it.'

---

25 *After purchase the Sea Maas was converted to take the same type of hydraulic gantry crane as the 400-tonners like the Polarlight. After this she had a cargo capacity of around 600 tonnes – about five times that of the Lady Morven.*

The author is seen here testing out the travelling gantry crane after its fitting to *Glencloy* (V). These hydraulically operated machines were very flexible and adaptable (including the ability to pick up loose timber logs) and ideal for the variety of cargoes that were the staple of the West Highland trade.

He apologised then and took the boat safely into port. I signed his docket, bade him farewell and scored him off my Christmas card list.

The next big thing to hit the coasters was the medical examinations. All the skippers, mates, engineers, and eventually AB's had to have valid medical certificates. Each certificate complimented the other. If you had no medical you could not revalidate your certificate of service, etc. The first time I went for a medical the Board of Trade doctor was busy, so I got a young doctor who passed me no bother. The only thing he said was to watch my weight, which at that time was about 18 stones, and issued the certificate for two years. Two years later my weight was still the same and as my skippers' ticket was due to be revalidated in a few months time, I went for my medical.

This time I got the proper doctor who did a really thorough examination; soles of the feet to the top of the head. The last two things he did were to take my height and weight. He then asked me to sit down whilst he was scribbling with some figures on a scrap bit of paper. I glanced across at my chart which looked good. Heart, lungs, eyesight, hearing, teeth all had ticks. I felt confident about passing. Nothing had changed in two years. He had finished his scribbling.

'You are grossly overweight, even allowing for the maximum percentage allowance which would put you at sixteen stones. You are two stone two pounds over that. For your height and build your ideal weight should be thirteen and a half stones. What are you going to do about it?'

'Well, I was eighteen stone two years ago and your colleague passed me then. I still feel the same now as I did then.' I said meekly. It is only small coasters I am on. We only trade round the islands. We are never far out from land.'

'My colleague should never have passed you then, sorry. But you have failed the medical. I will give you a certificate for three months. I won't stop you going to sea. If you don't lose two stones in the next three months, don't come back to this surgery because I will fail you again.'

I paid the medical fee, took my certificate and slipped out of his surgery. I went home and called into my local and had about ten pints of Guinness and then went to the Chinese carry out and ordered ribs, curry, rice and chips. The diet was to start next day.

For the next three months I changed my diet completely; no chocolate, no fry-ups, no beer. This was a nightmare situation to be in, especially at sea. When the crew were making the breakfast the waft of bacon sizzling in the pan would reach the wheelhouse and torture my taste buds. I would then picture my early days as deckhand. The frying pan on, bacon, sausages, black pudding, fried eggs, delicious! Coming on watch, I had cornflakes, milk, no sugar, toast, marmalade, no butter. Cruel, really cruel! Sometimes my fellow skippers would call up on the radio,

'How's the diet going McGinn? Still off the fry-ups? We were ashore last night, had a few pints and went to an Indian restaurant. You would have enjoyed it. It was buffet night. Eat as much as you like for a fiver. Aye, it was a really good night McGinn. I think we are having lamb chops tonight, followed by ice cream and fruit. What are you having?'

'Bastards!' I would shout back, 'I'll get my own back someday.'

I did manage to lose two stones and went back and passed the medical for two years. The doctor was really nice to me this time and basically checked my heart, took my weight and that was it. I was just 16 stones. To tell the truth I did feel a lot fitter. I wasn't as short of breath and I could walk faster. There was a feel-good factor about it. I did put on some weight for a while but always managed to reach the target in time for the medical. One or two of the older men failed the medical and had to go ashore which was a shame as they only had a couple of years to go until retiring age. Everything had become a matter of rules and regulations.

CHAPTER 36

The Last of the Puffers

One time when out on one of the islands with a small cargo of coal I was coming back from telephoning the office when this old woman stopped me.

'Are you the skipper of the puffer at the pier?'

'Yes, that's right,' I replied.

'I see you have one of these new fangled things for discharging the cargo.'

'Oh, you mean the crane and grab. The days when men shovelled coal into tubs are long gone. Men just won't do it now. It's a lot quicker, faster turn round.'

'My son tells me you will be away again tonight. Everybody is in a hurry now. Rushing here, rushing there. I remember when the old puffers came in years ago. They were in for at least two days. We knew all the crews by their first names.'

She mentioned a few skipper's names. Some I had heard of but didn't know. It was long before my time.

'It was like a holiday when the puffer was in. Us youngsters would rush from school, have something to eat and go down and drive the horse and cart for my father and have a laugh with the crew. There were some real characters on the boats in those days. Always good for a laugh. Everywhere is changing and not always for the better. Nobody has any time to talk now. Conversation has died away. It's all television now. Have you got television on board?'

'Oh, aye. But we only get a picture now and again. It's not worth bothering with. I haven't seen Coronation Street for years,' I said to her.

'Talking about television, that reminds me the 'Undersea World of Jacques Cousteau' is on at eleven o'clock. I like to watch it. Cheerio!'

With that she went back into the house. What a nice old woman. I later found out that she was 90 years of age. She certainly didn't look it and what a great memory she had. A lot of what the old woman said was true. The puffers gave a service to the community and now they are no more. Cash is king. People don't matter.

That's the way I saw it in the last two or three years of the existence of the company I worked for. It was not the company's fault that the puffer trade died. The bosses fought like hell to keep the firm going and save our jobs. Maybe if the government had stepped in with a cash injection the puffers/coasters would have survived and would still be trading round the islands. Who knows?

By December 1994 all the boats were tied up and by the 6th January 1995 we were paid off. One hundred and fifty years of giving a service to the West Coast and Islands had come to an end, never to return. It was very sad. The small puffer *Eilean Easdale* ceased trading about the same date[26] and her crew should be included here as they were also among 'The Last of the Puffermen'.

26 November 1994

Epilogue

It was the Conservative government's refusal to renew the Tariff Rebate Subsidy for bulk shipping to the Highlands and Islands for 1995 and beyond that left the Board of Glenlight Shipping with no alternative but to withdraw from servicing the remote West Coast communities. Negotiations over this matter were protracted and widely publicised in the press and television.

That single shift in policy spelt the death knell for the puffers.

Once the pride of the puffer fleet, *Pibroch II* (1956) lies abandoned and dilapidated on the west coast of Ireland. In these days of global warming and the need to get goods traffic off the roads where are she and her sisters when we most need them? (*Photo courtesy of Jack Moran*)